The Book of
Stogumber, Monksilver, Nettlecombe & Elworthy

A Portrait of Four Parishes
Maurice & Joyce Chidgey

HALSGROVE

First published in Great Britain in 2003

British Library Cataloguing-in-Publication Data
A CIP record for this title is available from the British Library

ISBN 1 84114 246 8

HALSGROVE

Halsgrove House
Lower Moor Way
Tiverton, Devon EX16 6SS
Tel: 01884 243242
Fax: 01884 243325
email: sales@halsgrove.com
website: www.halsgrove.com

Frontispiece photograph: *Nettlecombe Court and the Church of the Blessed Virgin Mary from the Park, c.1905.
Unfortunately the lady has not been identified – she was probably a member of the Trevelyan family.*

Printed and bound in Great Britain by CPI Bath Press, Bath

Foreword

by Denis Davis, whose family have been
associated with the four parishes for 200 years.

Despite having to forsake my native heath – initially through a call to arms and subsequently in the pursuit of a career – my affection for West Somerset has prevailed. As both Hazel, my wife, and I were brought up at Monksilver, wherever 'outrageous fortune' took us, we had at least one thing in common. Thus we were able to console ourselves when necessary by reminiscing about 'old times'. These, since they were mostly pleasant, centred upon the contention that we had enjoyed an interesting, sound, nay often idyllic, childhood. Many people, celebrities amongst them, assert that a deprived upbringing was the catalyst that spurred them to succeed. In my instance it was certainly the opposite. We drank spring water that surely was like wine, ate golden butter from a pure Channel Islands herd and always had good meat and lovely fresh vegetables.

Unfettered access to entrancing countryside, and involvement with domestic needs and with wildlife, promoted values within us that many sadly lack today. We could go where the fancy took us without fear of harm. In a community (one honestly worthy of such an appellation) there was, too, a fascination with the interesting, often eccentric characters who pervaded the scene – alas, now all gone!

Maurice and Joyce Chidgey are to be congratulated on placing under one cover this quartet, most meticulously researched, heightening the nostalgia and encouraging half-forgotten memories to fuller recall. In a world which now suffers from a sameness wherever one may travel, in turning these pages we can exclaim with real justification, 'Ah, those were the days!'

Scott's Cottage dating from the mid-Jacobean
period (1640–70) at Yarde. The pump was installed c.1820.

Above: *Zinch Cottage, one of Stogumber's oldest dwellings, c.1930.*

Top right: *Willett Tower, 1937.*

Right: *The Nettlecombe valley from Fair Cross with Yarde in the foreground.*

Below: *Stogumber looking from Hillhead, late 1940s.*

Contents

Harvest time at Monksilver, 1936.

Above: *Clearing the road from Huish Barton to Chidgley after freezing rain brought down branches and telegraph wires, 1947.*

Inset: *Harry Ford, cowman at Nettlecombe Court in the 1930s. He was also an expert slaughterer and dresser of deer; he lived at Yarde Mill House.*

Grinding swedes in a field above Stogumber, 1946. Left to right: Gordon, Roger and Percy Hutchings.

Acknowledgements

In this book we have attempted to portray village life, the ways of this historic countryside and some of the personalities who have added colour to this beautiful area down through the years. We are very appreciative of all the help, kindness and hospitality shown during its compilation, without which publication would not have been possible. We have made every effort to be accurate using the information received, but apologise in the event of any errors or omissions. We would like to express our sincere thanks to the present and former people of the four parishes covered, which make up a very special corner of West Somerset. It is your book – we hope that you enjoy it!

We gratefully acknowledge the following for the loan of photographs, other material and information: Dennis Clarke, Flossie Hall, David Beach, Judy Bryant, Gordon and Olive Yeo, Ken Stephens, Mary Jenkins, Stogumber Cricket Club, Darby Ash, Carol Parsons, Emma Stark, Charles Brundrett, Lesley Morgan, Clare Thomas, Roy Dennett, Robin Bex, Sandra Moore, Ron Penny, Bill and Carol Marke, Jill Smith, Revd Elfrida Savigear, Audrey Scrace, David and Ann Bryant, S. Nash, Vivian Brewer, Valerie Stevens, Marjorie Hann, Geoffrey Day, Charles Williams, Sandra Hull, Judith Illman, Sheila Webb, Jeff Criddle, Dennis Symes, Steve Guscott, Phil Watts (Williton), Robin Wichard, W.A.C. Theed, Philip Blackmore, Phil Watts (Nailsea), Bob Reed Collection, Heather Tennant, W.R.G. West, Mike Hayes, John Lillington, Eric Clavey, Joan Jones, Tim and Max Richmond, Peter Williamson, Ernie Nicholls, John Bryant, Kathleen Sellick, Rodney Somerfield, John Burns, Barbara Vearncombe, Mrs A. Sanders, Debbie Quinn (head of Stogumber CEVC First School), Terry and Myfanwy Squires, Brian Kirk, Richard Ninis, Dr J.H. Crothers, Sonia Wylds, Jim White, Bryan Cliff (EMN Community Hall), Charlie and Barbara Jewell, David and Shirley Sully, David Winkley, Bonnie Bindon, Robert Notley, Jill Gillman, Jill Sellick, Andrew and Christine Howe, Barbara Howe, Mary Scott, Mrs D. Gliddon, Derek Quint (Kwinty, *see cartoon p.23*), David Hosegood, Doreen Morse, Richard Chamberlain, Jack Bryant, Leonard Wills Field Studies Centre, Rita Lang, George Tuckfield, Peter Notley, Dr Katherine Wyndham, Nigel and Wendy Cavey, the estate of Mrs Beatrice Taylor, Derek Watts, Bill Cheek, Air Pic, Victor Ambrus, Keith Norcutt, Beaulieu National Motor Museum, Audrey Takel, Angela Rigby, Frank Stevens, Rosemary Cox MBE, Emily Stephens, Richard Denot, Beryl Simms, Violet Woods, Sheila Prescott, Judith Sherren, Susan Hill, Mary Green, Alistair and Sarah Cade (Notley Arms), Dr Glyn Court.

Special thanks for assistance are due to Denis Davis, Ron and Honor Hayes, Christine and the late Geoff Hayes, Daisy Tuckfield, Fred Hutchings, Hector Potter, Roger and June Hutchings, Vera Chidgey and Celia Vardy. Thanks also to the editor of the *West Somerset Free Press* and the Somerset Record Office.

Two maps are reproduced from the *Victoria County History, Somerset V*, pp112 and 176, by permission of the General Editor, also one photograph and a line drawing from Halsgrove publications *Murder and Mystery on Exmoor* and *Legends of Exmoor*, and two maps by permission of Ordnance Survey.

Lastly, we extend our grateful thanks to Naomi Cudmore, who lives in the parish of Nettlecombe and is Commissioning Editor of the Halsgrove Community History Series, for her advice and help. We also wish her God speed when she embarks from Southampton next year on the Global Challenge of 2004–5, 'the world's toughest yacht race'.

Maurice and Joyce Chidgey, 2003

Above: *Iron-ore miners at West Adit, Colton Pit, 1908.*

Left: *Nettlecombe Court and Parish Church, c.1890.*

Below: *Combe Sydenham Hall from the rear, c.1950.*

Introduction

Like most of West Somerset, the four parishes of Stogumber, Monksilver, Nettlecombe and Elworthy are primarily agricultural, in spite of the industry having its fair share of problems in recent years. With the great changes in agricultural methods, far fewer workers are now employed on the land and some farms have diversified, especially since the national foot-and-mouth epidemic in 2001. Despite this the area still produces fine crops, sheep and cattle – such as the pedigree herd of Charolais at Escott Farm, near Stogumber.

Situated partly within the Exmoor National Park, tourism also features in this area with welcoming pubs, resting places, eating houses and tea gardens. The landscape is punctuated with fine mansions and quaint whitewashed cottages, which hold the key to curious legends and fascinating stories alike.

The big employers of the old days – the large estates and the iron-ore mines – have long gone, but parishioners are showing resilience in changing times to ensure a bright future in their panoramic surroundings. Among the communal achievements over the years have been the Village Hall at Stogumber and, more recently, the Elworthy, Monksilver and Nettlecombe Community Hall at Monksilver and the magnificent cricket ground and pavilion at Stogumber.

Ecclesiastically, the four parishes form part of the Quantock Towers Benefice, which comprises Bicknoller, Crowcombe, Monksilver, Nettlecombe, Sampford Brett, Stogumber and Elworthy (redundant). The priest-in-charge is the Revd Elfrida Savigear, whose rectory is at Bicknoller. Civically, all four parishes fall within West Somerset District, with a total population in 2001 of 1,100. The only remaining functional local school is at Stogumber, which still flourishes with a healthy number of pupils engaging in a wide range of activities.

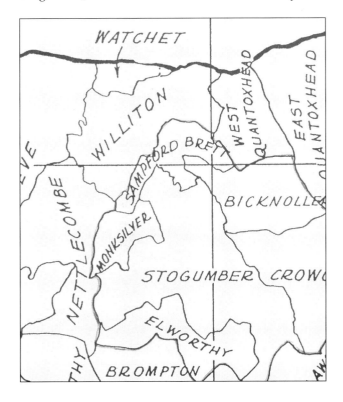

The Revd Elfrida Beatrice Savigear, priest-in-charge of the four parishes covered in this book, which form part of the Quantock Towers Benefice. She was inducted in February 1999, being the first female priest of the seven parishes in the united benefice.

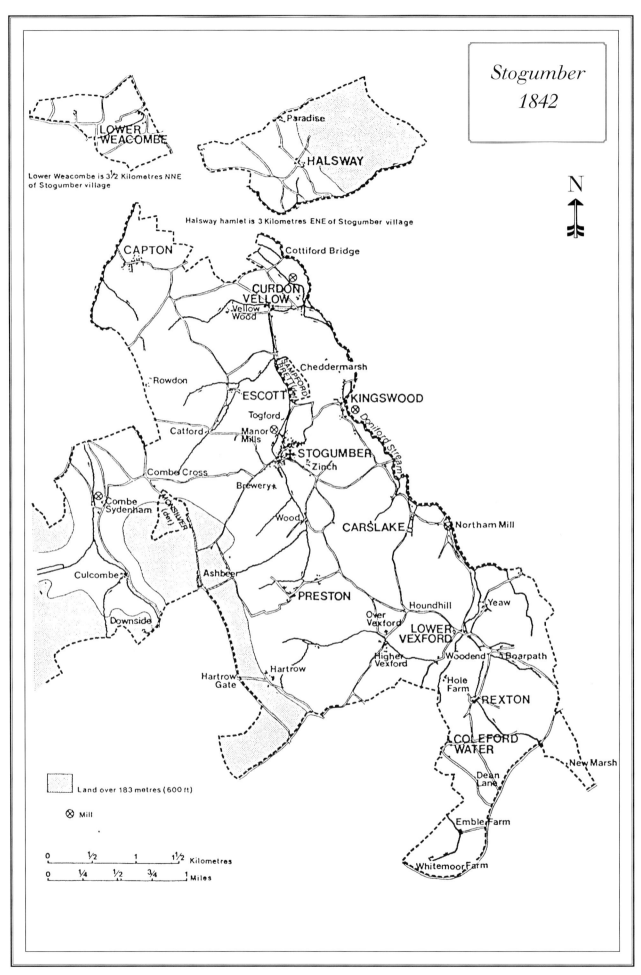

Stogumber
1842

N

Lower Weacombe is 3½ Kilometres NNE of Stogumber village

LOWER WEACOMBE

Paradise

HALSWAY

Halsway hamlet is 3 Kilometres ENE of Stogumber village

CAPTON

Cottiford Bridge

CURDON
VELLOW

Yellow
Wood

Rowdon

Cheddermarsh

ESCOTT

KINGSWOOD

Togford

Catford

Manor
Mills

STOGUMBER

Zinch

Combe Cross

Brewery

Combe
Sydenham

Wood

CARSLAKE

Northam Mill

Culcombe

Ashbeer

PRESTON

Houndhill

Yeaw

Over
Vexford

LOWER
VEXFORD

Downside

Higher
Vexford

Woodend

Boarpath

Hartrow
Gate

Hartrow

Hole
Farm

REXTON

COLEFORD
WATER

New Marsh

Dean
Lane

Land over 183 metres (600 ft)

⊗ Mill

Emble Farm

Whitemoor Farm

0   ½   1   1½   Kilometres
0   ¼   ½   ¾   1   Miles

One

Stogumber

The picturesque village of Stogumber lies serenely situated in the valley between the Brendon and Quantock Hills. To the north is the Bristol Channel and to the south spreads the broad and fertile Vale of Taunton Deane. From any direction, the only route to Stogumber is by way of winding roads and steep, narrow lanes which make their way through the lush countryside. The rich red soil of the fields can be seen after ploughing, but the pastures are bright green, and the parish prides itself on its many fine farms. Approaching Stogumber from the north, one passes Curdon, which previously boasted a smithy as well as two mills, and Vellow with its riverside tea garden and pottery (formerly a forge at one time worked by five smiths). One then arrives at Stogumber with its gracious old houses and quaint cottages built of cob or local red sandstone, into which blend the newer developments such as Deane Close and Sawpits Close.

Behind this peaceful façade lies a vibrant community. Among the many village events eagerly anticipated is the open-gardens weekend in June, the proceeds from which are given to various local charities and the Parish Church. Dedicated to St Mary the Virgin, the church lies just off the Square at the top of a hill, with its red sandstone tower, begun in the thirteenth century, rising majestically heavenwards. The large church stands on a prominent and dominating site, south of the old market-place, with the medieval former vicarage house (now a private residence) to the west. A new rectory was built in 1987. The former rectory estate, the lands of the probable Saxon minster, seems to have been concentrated north and east of the church.

There were nine separate estates in Stogumber parish recorded in the Domesday Book, including one belonging to the church. Later, the two distinct manors of Stogumber Rectory and Stogumber emerged.

The Parish Church has been the focal point of village life for six centuries, and even in Norman times there was a place of worship on this site, known in 1086 as the Church of St Mary of Warverdinestoch. In about 1400 the church was partially destroyed by fire. The lower stages of the tower, the westerly bay and south porch survived and were incorporated in the rebuilding and enlargement. The church's six bells, which weigh just less than three tons and are rung regularly, bear the following dates: 1624, 1687, 1745, 1755, 1857 and 1880. In 1764 a weathercock was purchased at a cost of 10s.6d. and a new clock was obtained in 1792 for £14.5s.0d.; this was re-gilded in 1997. The church registers were started in 1559, but the list of vicars dates back to 1249. The church plate includes a chalice of 1615 and a paten and flagon of 1733.

The living became a vicarage in the patronage of the Wells Chapter in 1291 and remained so until 1977 when it became a curacy-in-charge with Monksilver, Nettlecombe and Brompton Ralph. In 2000 Stogumber became part of the Quantock Towers Benefice.

The Baptist Chapel at Stogumber was founded by Christopher Hawkins in 1690; before this date a man named Hugh Duddridge had preached in various parish farmhouses. In 1729 land was purchased and the first church was constructed. In time, this was outgrown by the congregation, and the present building was erected on the same site in 1868 at a cost of £410. This chapel was closed in 1990 and subsequently purchased by Stogumber Arts Ltd as a venue for the visual and performing arts. The building is listed, with specific reference being made to the high quality of the railings. It has developed into a popular Arts Centre, which is used primarily for music and drama, but which also serves as an ideal venue for art exhibitions – and as home to the Chapel Arts Choir, which has an extensive repertoire and performs both within and beyond the village. The success of the Arts Centre has been due largely to the artistic direction of Colin and Vera Metters, and is typical of what can be achieved by the commitment, enthusiasm and spirit of the village.

In 2001 Stogumber's population stood at 660, but the parish once boasted a much larger community, topping 1,500 in 1850. The 1851 census listed a draper, milliner, dressmakers, shoemakers, building workers, several retailers and professional men, including a carrier and a veterinary surgeon. Within living memory the village was self-supporting, and

Left: *Manor House, Stogumber, c.1905.*

Bottom left and right: *Dr Mary Meyers and Dr Roy Meyers.*

Below: *The doctors' surgery (now Manor Cottage), c.1950s.*

had three inns and several shops. There was the Swan Inn (now Swan House in High Street) and the Dragon Inn (now Lauriston House), which became the George Inn after a fire in 1752 and closed about 1800. The White Horse is the only surviving public house, dating back to at least 1680. Earlier there was a Red Lion Inn established by 1668 and the Ram or Black Ram by 1684, as well as a 'drinkhouse' at Vellow in 1619, none of which survived.

The earliest settlements were largely established beside the valley watercourses which feed the Doniford stream. Originally the village was called Walver-de-Stoke and was a royal Saxon possession, but following the Norman Conquest, and the arrival of Gomer, the Norman, Walver-de-Stoke became Stoke-de-Gomer – Stogumber.

In medieval times Stogumber appears to have been the wool town for a large area. Later, the collecting place for the sale of wool was apparently the old freestanding Markethouse, built about 1800 and amalgamated with the White Horse Inn during the 1860s. The loss of this cottage industry heralded a period of relative poverty locally, from which it took the community a long time to recover.

The three 'big' houses of the parish – Combe Sydenham, Hartrow and Halsway – would have employed a large number of staff, with many living in, and the local farms would also have employed a great many people. The Trevelyan estate covered as much as one-third of the parish by the sixteenth century and more land at Vellow was acquired in 1520.

There were two main routes through the parish in the late-seventeenth century – from Bridgwater to Barnstaple and from Taunton to Watchet and Minehead. A new road from Crowcombe through Bicknoller to Williton in 1807 reduced the volume of traffic passing through Stogumber and left the village isolated from the main routes.

A workhouse was established in 1752, where in 1769 there were 25 residents, including children. In 1836 the parish became part of the Williton Poor Law Union, with the local workhouse being given up by 1840. Stogumber has a Parish Council and was part of the Williton Rural District from 1894–1974, thereafter becoming part of West Somerset District. In 1629 there was an unlicensed schoolmaster, and in 1769 pauper children were being taught at the expense of the parish. Stogumber Baptist Chapel established a school in the late-eighteenth century which in 1803 occupied a building attached to the chapel. Supported by voluntary contributions, by 1818 it was providing an education for 30 boys from the poorer classes, but seems to have closed around the 1840s. Seven years earlier, however, in 1833, the National School had opened its doors, and by 1840 occupied a site near Zinch; in 1846 pupils on the roll numbered 103, rising to 162 in 1879. From 1840–90 there was also a boarding- and day-school for young ladies at Mill Close. In 1900 Mr G.P. Fevre became head of the National School and by 1902 there were five teachers and 118 children on the school roll. At the time of the school's centenary, which was celebrated in 1933, there were some 80 children attending under Mr Fevre and his two assistants.

From 1971 the older children travelled to Williton, with Stogumber becoming a First School for the 5–9-year-olds. The school survived threats of closure in the 1960s and 1980s due to lack of numbers and celebrated its 150th anniversary in 1983. Pupil numbers then increased and it is hoped that this trend will continue for many years to come.

Around 1910 Stogumber had a resident police-man by the name of PC Bodger, whose home is now known as Asthall Cottage. Behind this cottage was the old village lock-up which, until some years ago, still had chains attached to the walls. The cottage was also used as a dentist's surgery, and amongst its former residents was authoress Margaret Maddocks. Brig House in Vellow Road was built to replace this police house (brig being naval slang for lock-up). This also is no longer a police house as there has been no resident policeman in the village since the 1970s, the last being PC John Ribbons.

Neither have there been any resident practising physicians since the 1970s, the last being Drs Roy and Mary Meyers, of Manor House, who had a surgery in Manor Cottage. (Dr Mary was also a magistrate, sitting on the former Williton Bench.)

At Lower Preston Farm, which was reputed to have been a nunnery, there is said to have existed an underground passage connecting with nearby Hartrow Manor; from time to time farm machinery

A steam train entering Stogumber station, 1989.

Above: *Asthall Cottage (the early police house), 2002.*

Left: *Entrance to the old Stogumber lock-up at the former police house (Asthall Cottage).*

being used in the fields between Hartrow and Lower Preston reputedly sank into what appeared to have been an old passageway.

In the far north of the civil parish lies the hamlet of Capton. In 1066 the manor of Capton was held by Earl Harold, and by the late-thirteenth century was occupied by the Raleghs of Nettlecombe, whose land extended southwards from here by the 1280s; at this time the estate was known as the manor of Rowdon with a manor-house which, by 1334, included an oratory. Like Nettlecombe manor, Rowdon manor descended through the Ralegh and Trevelyan fami-lies, although it was not referred to as a manor after 1823. A secondary house has also been built on the site.

A building in the grounds of Capton House was converted for use as a Methodist chapel in 1840 and services were held regularly there until 1916. An orchard at Capton Farm was called the Skittle Alley in 1840, and there was a smithy at Capton during the nineteenth century. Red sandstone was quarried in the hamlet until closure around 1912, but the quarry was reopened in 1993. Its hard red sandstone has been extensively used locally and can be seen, for example, in the facing of Minehead sea wall for a stretch of one-and-a-quarter miles, as well as in homes next to the old St Peter's School at Williton.

Being part of the West Somerset Railway, Stogumber's railway station is situated at the parish boundary near Kingswood. Initially laid between Taunton and Watchet and run by the Bristol and Exeter Railway, the line was officially opened on 5 April 1862, being extended to Minehead in 1874 under the banner of the Great Western Railway. A Railway Inn (now closed) was built near Stogumber Station in 1880. In 1882 the 7ft wide-gauge track was reduced to 4ft 8$\frac{1}{2}$ins narrow gauge. The change-over was completed between the last train on the Saturday evening and the first train on the Monday morning, about 500 workmen being involved.

The railway was taken over by British Railways in 1947 and in January 1971 the Taunton to Minehead line was closed, but a new private West Somerset Railway company was formed which opened a service from Minehead to Stogumber in 1978. This was extended to Bishops Lydeard a year later and is the longest in the country offering steam services. The company's ambition is to have a permanent service into Taunton.

The site for Stogumber Station was carved out of the old sandstone hillside, with the station buildings on the north side of the single-line track and the raised platform (originally wooden but now replaced by concrete) perched above the Doniford stream. Over the years, scores of Stogumber parishioners have walked the lanes to catch trains for their work, shopping and schools at Taunton and Minehead, as also have many tourists keen to take advantage of the line's scenic route.

✤ *Village Views* ✤

Above and right: *Views of Stogumber from Oldway, c.1920.*
Background image: *Aerial view of Stogumber.*

Left: *In the year 2000 the hamlet of Kingswood, near Stogumber, celebrated the renovation of its Victorian village pump with a traditional 'well dressing' ceremony. Pictured are Brian Heaton and the Revd Elfrida Savigear.*

Left: *High Street, Stogumber, with the Swan Inn (now a private residence) on the left, c.1920. The building on the right is known as Seven Crosses and was once a sweet shop; its thatched roof was removed and the walls raised to provide an upper floor c.1928. It was sold for £100 in the late 1920s by the Revd Ambrose Couch (the vicar at Stogumber for 36 years) to raise money for the building of Church House (now the Village Hall).*

Right: *Seven Crosses, High Street, Stogumber, 2002, showing its crosses and raised roof. The origin of the crosses is speculative.*

Below: *The Square, Stogumber, c.1920s.*

Below right: *The Square in the 1950s.*

An Edwardian scene in Station Road, Stogumber, showing Mullins' shop on the right and the old police house in the background.

Above and above right: *Brook Street, c.1910 and c.1975.*

Right: *Icicles hanging from High Street roofs at Stogumber, 1963. The boys are David and Graham Williams.*

Below: *View of Stogumber Railway Station from Braglands Cross, late 1940s.*

Right: *The Almonry, c.1985. The late Sir Oliver Barnett, QC, is seen walking his dog. Sir Oliver, who lived at the Almonry until his death in 1995, was Judge Advocate General from 1963–68. He was awarded the OBE in 1946, appointed CBE in 1954, took silk in 1956 and was knighted in 1968. In 2003 Lady Barnett still lives at the Almonry, which originally consisted of six small alms cottages built by the Sydenham estate to house six poor widows.*

Right: *Hill Street, Stogumber, c.1920s, showing Wynes Cottage (1611, formerly a farmhouse) and stable below.*

Below: *Hill Street, Stogumber, c.1950s, showing the old stable below Wynes Cottage converted into Fairlands Cottage, first lived in by Tom Besley and his parents. The Besleys were well known in the village and surrounding district as fish-mongers.*

Below right: *Wayshill (formerly known as The Knoll), Stogumber.*

Above: *Demolition of the Village Hut, 1990.*

Right: *The sawpit which was under the demolished Village Hut, adjacent to the present Sawpits Close.*

Stogumber children's Christmas party at the Village Hut, 1966.

Aerial view of Zinch House, Stogumber, c.1970.

Zinch

Nestling at the head of a valley to the south of Stogumber lies Zinch, a medieval farmhouse surrounded by around four acres of boundaried land. These boundaries consist of an outer ditch, a bank and an inner ditch and are separated into three distinct areas. It has been suggested by archaeologists that the boundaries might indicate an early settlement site, and in view of the topographical position this seems very probable.

Situated at the head of a valley that looks north-west, the site is very secluded and is hidden from all directions. Anyone approaching from the coast would have to come up the valley, passing Iron-Age Curdon camp at the mouth, and this, together with the natural shelter from the weather, abundance of springs and fertile soil, makes it an ideal spot to settle. It was no surprise, therefore, when proof of Iron-Age habitation turned up in the form of a piece of loom weight (identified by John Allen, of Exeter University), which was brought to the surface, along with some early pottery, during a winter of vigorous mole activity in the garden!

The church is situated on a promontory site 400 metres to the south-west of Zinch, and it would seem likely that this had been a religious site well before the Christians built the first church here; the village then grew up around the north and west of the church. There has been much discussion about the unusual name; after fairly extensive research and many suggestions from various experts, the most popular theory is that Zinch (also 'Zentes', meaning thorns) is Old English, meaning 'Land to the South of Stoke'.

Although Zinch is now thought of as being within the village of Stogumber, it was once part of the manor of Over Vexford and the Manor Courts were probably held here. (The area in front of the present house is called 'Court Front', and listed in the inventory of buildings at Zinch is the 'court old room'.)

One of the earliest deeds that mentions Zinch (Zentes) dates from 1383 when John Roche, of Vexford, leased Zinch, Vexford, Rexton and Hole in Stogumber parish and Boleworthy in Exton parish to William Whitchurch and Thomas Pange. Prior to this the deeds refer to Vexford Superior and this may or may not include Zinch.

When the present house was built is uncertain since the timbers are of elm and there is no database as yet to allow dendrodating to determine the felling dates of the timber. The house was built using jointed crucks that stand on posts which in turn stand on stone 'plates', indicating an earlier construction date, but how early is a matter for argument! The house, detached kitchen and other buildings are joined together by a wall, forming a compact courtyard plan, which was common in Saxon farmsteads. Evidence of the site being used for industrial purposes has been found beside a leat that runs along one of the boundaries. In this area it is not unusual to pick up pieces of slag, often intermingled with lime, and the odd piece of iron ore.

Over Vexford was held by William Franklin in 1242 and a William Franklin conveyed it to Richard de la Roche in 1309, his son Simon inheriting the manor of Over Vexford in 1318. The ownership of Zinch passed from Simon de la Roche down to John Roche a century or so later; he then left the property in trust to Jacobus (John) Luttrell, who died in 1403. One of the Roche heirs came along some years later and laid claim to the properties (since John Luttrell only had the lands in trust). Elizabeth Luttrell had quite a fight on her hands to prove that her family were the rightful owners.

Zinch was eventually sold to Sir William Wyndham in 1709 and inherited through marriage by the Earl of Egremont some time before 1796. In a deed dated 1715, Zinch is described as being near Stogumber town in the manor of Over Vexford. The Earl died in 1845 without an heir to the title and his properties became the subject of a battle for legal ownership that ultimately resulted in the sale of the property to the tenant, village craftsman John Sully.

In June 2003 Zinch House became the focal point for Britain's archaeology buffs when TV's Channel 4 'Time Team' conducted a special televised dig there. Zinch House was chosen live on TV from sites across the country as the one with the most archaeological potential. The Team discovered pottery dating back to Norman times, the remains of a Saxon-Norman home and flints which might mean the site could be prehistoric.

Duck before entering! One of the ancient doorways at Zinch.

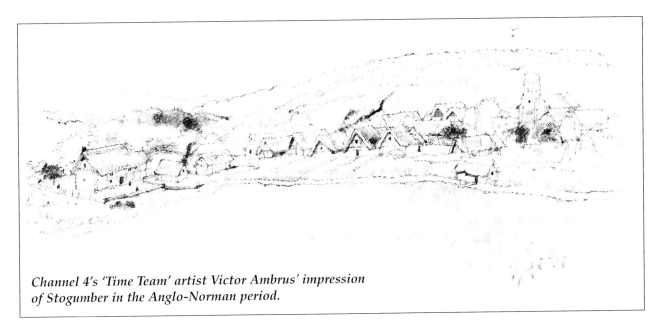

Channel 4's 'Time Team' artist Victor Ambrus' impression of Stogumber in the Anglo-Norman period.

Hartrow

Hartrow lies close to the south-west border of the parish of Stogumber and is mentioned in the Domesday Book. A corn-mill was recorded in 1086 and it is reputed that in medieval times there was a small village here, which survived to the late-sixteenth century. It was held by Ulwold in 1066 and 20 years later by Roger de Lisieux of William de Mohun, whose honour of Dunster it remained until around 1627. The first family named 'Hartrow' to hold the fee was that of William Hartrow in 1330 and it remained with them until 1475 when John Sydenham of Orchard took it over. The Sydenham family was connected with Hartrow for 88 years until 1563 when William Lacey purchased the remaining quarter share of the estate from John Sydenham of Combe.

Around 1580 a house is believed to have been built by William Lacey, fragments of which may have been included in an eighteenth-century wing of the north-west side of the present manor-house. To the south of this wing a hall was built in approximately 1817 and the main part of the house was replaced in 1830. Gothic additions to the great hall were made in the nineteenth century when medieval-style fittings and decorations were introduced. The hall was later adapted for use as a chapel.

Hartrow, with the Elworthy manor, remained in the Lacey family until 1695 when it passed to a married daughter, Sarah Rich, who, through her late son Thomas' estate, passed it on to Margaret Hay. On her death the estate passed to Margaret's sister Mary and in 1771 Mary's nephew, the Revd Bickham Escott, MP for Winchester, inherited it. In 1799 Bickham Escott died, leaving the estate to his three daughters, one of whom, Mary, married Thomas Sweet (later to be known as Sweet-Escott) and in 1811 they took possession of Hartrow Manor. It remained in the

Sweet-Escott family until 1936. It is reputed that a new park was established in 1816, replacing the earlier sixteenth-century one. Mr C. Thomas later bought the land and farmed it from Higher Vexford; the manor-house changed hands frequently in later years and in recent times has been further restored and cared for by its owners at the time of writing, Mr and Mrs Graham Sherren.

Following preaching in farmhouses of the parish by Hugh Duddridge from 1653, Christopher Hawkins established the Baptist Chapel at Stogumber in 1690, but only with the support and

The hall at Hartrow Manor, rebuilt by the Sweet-Escott family c.1817 incorporating Gothic windows, from a watercolour by Helena Maguire, 1894.

Hartrow Manor, 1948.

The dovecote at Hartrow, which is mentioned in the Domesday Book.

Far left: *Miss Sweet-Escott outside Hartrow on the day of her engagement, 1902.*

Bottom: *Scotch pine and cedar were planted at Hartrow in the 1600s. The cedar still stands, but the pine was blown down in 1991.*

protection of William Lacey, of Hartrow Manor, a Roman Catholic and county magistrate. During the reign of William and Mary, who were staunch Protestants, an angry mob set out from Taunton to burn down Hartrow Manor, but Christopher Hawkins heard of their intentions and impeded them, convincing them to return from whence they came peacefully, thus repaying the favour to William Lacey for his earlier support.

Thomas Rich was to be married in 1727 to Margaret Hay, daughter of the rector of Clatworthy, when he died at the early age of 24. It is said that on the evening before their wedding day the couple were busy preparing for the occasion when a coach and pair drew up outside. The groom-to-be was persuaded by the coachmen to accompany them to the coach. He was never seen alive again, having been robbed and killed by the villains. After the discovery of this event the grief-stricken bride-to-be had all the food, wine and presents locked away in an unused part of the house where they remained for many years. Her ghost is said to still roam around the house looking for her lost lover. The two men were caught and hanged from trees in the grounds, and on the anniversary of the event a headless coachman

drives the coach through the grounds! Later, a fine memorial to Thomas Rich was placed in Stogumber church by Margaret Hay and a paten and flagon, dated 1733, bearing the Hay coat of arms, was also presented; they are still in the church's possession.

During the 1920s and '30s Hartrow Manor was also used for the private tuition of students in preparation for their entrance examinations to Oxford and Cambridge Universities. Their tutor was Mr George Fevre, headmaster of Stogumber School, who specialised in mathematics.

Combe Sydenham

Situated within the Exmoor National Park, Combe Sydenham is a quarter of a mile south of Monksilver, but within the parish of Stogumber. The estate named Combe was held by Aelmer before 1066 and in 1086 by Thorgils of William de Mohun, but by the late-fourteenth century it had been renamed Combe Sydenham. Richard of Combe was said to occupy the land c.1240 and the estate was sold to Richard Sydenham, Justice of the Common Pleas, in 1367. The Sydenhams held the estate for approximately 284 years before it was confiscated in Parliamentary times as a punishment for the family's loyalty to the Crown. In 1653 Combe Sydenham was sold to John Ware, who later restored it to Sir John Posthumous Sydenham on instructions from the King after the Restoration. The whole estate was sold to George Musgrave in 1693 and remained in the Musgrave family until 1796 when the estate was sold to the Revd George Notley, of Chillington, South Somerset. Combe Sydenham remained in the Notley family until the 1950s when it was sold to Mr E.C. Campbell-Voullaire. The owner of the estate and hall at the time of writing is Mr W.A.C. Theed, who purchased it in 1964.

Squire Marwood Notley, of Combe Sydenham, c.1870.

Combe Sydenham Hall can be found nestling in the river valley between Monksilver and Elworthy. The original house was built by Sir John Sydenham in c.1360, but substantial alterations and rebuilding were carried out by Sir George Sydenham in 1580. At the top of the pilasters on either side of the porch can be seen Sir George's initials to the left and the date 1580 to the right. Above the porch is the Sydenham coat of arms and the window above the doorway is in the minstrels' gallery. In the top corners of the doorway appear the Sydenham ram, and also the bear, the family motif of Sir George Sydenham's wife Elizabeth, who came from Hailes in Gloucestershire; their initials can be seen in the vaulted ceiling.

The ground plan of the house was E-shaped in common with many Elizabethan houses; four towers – two large and two small – which surround the rear courtyard were added but only one remains today. The east wing was probably demolished by Cromwell's troops to slight the house as punishment for the family's Royalist loyalties.

In the mid-seventeenth century further remodelling of Combe Sydenham was carried out. By the nineteenth century the north of the court had been removed to make way for the new stables and coach-house which was built to the north-east of the house, the west wing was partly refitted with a new staircase put into the base of the western tower and the roofs and most of the windows were renewed.

The Gatehouse Tower has been recreated using an earlier picture, but the stone arch was reputed to have been built around 1450. The water-powered corn-mill was mentioned in the Domesday Book, and while modern restoration was taking place in the 1980s larger wheels installed over a period of about 1,000 years were discovered.

The 500-acre estate has a Deer Park which was established by the seventeenth century; in 1911 this ran to 13 acres and was stocked with red and fallow deer. Today it holds a large herd of fallow deer. Around the Deer Park are restored wrought-iron railings which had probably survived the last war's iron collections through being hidden, following collapse, by overgrown brambles.

In the estate grounds are six ponds, some of which date back to at least Elizabethan times and from which it is reputed that water leats were constructed for field irrigation in the late-sixteenth century.

Further up the valley, the settlement of Goodley, now deserted, is thought to have been decimated by the 'Black Death'. John de Godele, a Dean of Wells Cathedral, was born at Goodley in the fourteenth century, and during Victorian times a farmhouse and cottage in the settlement were still occupied.

Of course, with a house of Combe Sydenham's age, legends are inevitable and while it is true that Elizabeth Sydenham – the only one of Sir George's children to survive into adulthood – and the famous Sir Francis Drake did marry, it is a cannonball which is at the centre of the legend. There are variations to the tale, one of which follows.

While Elizabeth Sydenham was a maid-of-honour at the court of Queen Elizabeth I she met Sir Francis Drake and they fell deeply in love. Although her parents, Sir George and Lady Elizabeth, were opposed to the romance, having preferred for their daughter a local wealthy suitor, the couple became engaged. Before they could get married, Drake was off again on one of his long voyages to distant shores, leaving Elizabeth at home to await his return. After many years had elapsed, there was still no word from Drake and rumours were spread that he and his crew had perished. Elizabeth was coerced by her parents to marry another suitor and to this she agreed, although in her heart of hearts she was sure that Sir Francis was still alive and loved her. Wedding preparations were made and the ceremony was to take place in the Parish Church at Stogumber.

On the day of her wedding Elizabeth, still convinced that Sir Francis was alive, offered up a

Left: *South-east view of Combe Sydenham Hall.*

Inset: *Drake's cannonball at Combe Sydenham Hall.*

Below left: *Montague Notley, of Combe Sydenham, c.1900.*

Below: *Combe Sydenham Hall, 1783.*

Left: *Estate shoot at Combe Sydenham, c.1900. Left to right: ?, Marwood Notley, Keeper Snell, Montague Notley, ?.*

Meet at Combe Sydenham of the Nettlecombe Harriers, c.1905.

prayer asking for some sign to be made to her if it were so. As she was leaving the house on her way to the church, a cannonball landed in front of her. Believing this to be an omen from Sir Francis Drake, Elizabeth turned around and refused to go ahead with the arranged wedding ceremony.

Sir Francis Drake did, in fact, arrive back on English shores that day and ultimately married Elizabeth Sydenham in Monksilver Parish Church on 18 June 1583, she becoming his second wife. The weighty cannonball can still be seen at Combe Sydenham and it is said that Elizabeth regarded it as bringing her good luck – it might do the same for you if you touch it!

Another legend is that involving the exorcism of the devil from Combe Sydenham by bell, book and candle. The devil took the form of a black dog and a boy carried it in a bag and threw it into the fifth pond. Immediately the pond flared up in flaming brimstone and has been dry ever since!

The Sydenham Chapel in Stogumber Parish Church's south aisle is said to date from the sixteenth century and is separated from the rest of the church by a wrought-iron screen. The tomb of Sir George Sydenham, Sir Francis Drake's father-in-law, can be found here. The tomb chest shows Sir George with his two wives, one on either side of him, and at his feet are three small baby figures wrapped in swaddling-clothes and a kneeling adult figure, most probably his daughter Elizabeth. The carving of the tomb is amateurish and the year date omitted, but the canopy above the tomb and the pillars are more finely detailed. At Easter flowers are placed in the cupped hands of Lady Sydenham. Memorials to the Musgrave family can be seen on the walls of the chapel, as also is Sir Francis Drake's prayer used before the Battle of Cadiz in 1587, which reads:

O Lord God, when thou givest to thy servants to endeavour any great matter, grant us also to know that it is not the beginning, but the continuing of the same unto the end until it be thoroughly finished which yieldeth the true glory.

Combe Sydenham Ponds, c.1950.

Keeper's Cottage (far right) at Combe Sydenham, c.1910.

Combe Sydenham Hall with a view of dovecot (now demolished) through the archway, c.1800.

STOGUMBER CHURCH.

Above: *The Church of St Mary the Virgin, c.1920.*

Right: *Interior of St Mary's Church, c.1920.*

Below: *Restoration of the six Stogumber church bells, 1950.*

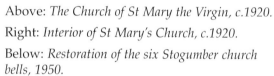

Right: *Sarah Sully (left), aged 95, and her sister Tish, 85, walking home from church in 1936. Sarah used a chair for support as she had fractured a leg.*

Right: *Choir of St Mary's Church, Stogumber, 1996. Left to right, back: Les Simms, Bruce Young, Geoff Hayes (choir member for 65 years); third row: Ellen Williamson, Ron Penny (choir member for over 60 years), Claire Rawle, Elsa Richards, Mary Green, Wendy Cavey, Mary Field (choirmistress), Monica Noakes, June Illingworth, Vera Metters, Rosemary Pester, David Leonard; second row: Natalie Cavey, Emily Cavey, Tom Turner, Jenny Matravers, Stephanie Cavey; front: Heather Frith, Thaddea Lock, Helen Matravers.*

Left: *After lying abandoned in Stogumber Bier House (which was sited in a modern-day garden at Sawpits Close) for more than 20 years, this bier was restored by parishioners to its original 1936 condition for display at the 1982 Stogumber Festival. In earlier years the church bier was the accepted mode of transport for the poorer departed in the country, whose families could not afford a farm wagon drawn by a team of horses. Unless you were the local squire or lord of the manor your coffin would have been man-powered from cottage or remote farm to the local church. This bier was made by E.J. Sully of Stogumber in 1936 at a cost of £36, less a discount of 20 per cent. It was hired out at 2s.6d., and for an extra 1s. a man would clean it before and after use.*

Above: *Bruce Young planting the millennium yew in Stogumber churchyard with staff and pupils of the local school, 2000.*

Left: *The south side of St Mary's, 2002.*

❧ *Baptists* ❧

The gate to Stogumber Baptist Chapel is on the right and the old Almshouses are in the background in this view from c.1912.

Inset: Group at a Stogumber Baptist Chapel outing, c.1940s.

Left: *In 1987 the Baptist Chapel said farewell to a member with loyal family links of 334 years. The departure of Miss Kay Duddridge to live with her niece in Birmingham ended an association which began with the formation of the church locally by Hugh Duddridge in 1653 when he preached in farmhouses. Miss Duddridge was born at Lower Preston Farm, Stogumber, and remembered Hangman's Oak at Heddon where her ancestor was executed by Judge Jefferies for preaching the Gospel of Christ in a local farmhouse. For many years Miss Duddridge led the Sunday School, which at one time had some 70 pupils, two of whom, Jack and Chris Sansom, were among those attending the farewell. Miss Duddridge has since passed away and the chapel closed in 1990, being purchased by Stogumber Arts in 1993. Left to right, back row: Peter Wilson (pastor), Kathryn Wilson, Andrew Camper; third row: Mrs Alice Bryant, Katie Giles, Mrs June Hutchings (treasurer); second row: Florence Duddridge, Ben Wilson, Gemma Wilson; front: Percy Bryant (deacon), Miss Kay Duddridge, Mrs Hilda Langdon, Jack and Chris Sansom.*

Below: *Stogumber Baptist Chapel, 1991.*

Right: *The Chapel Arts Choir at the 50th anniversary service for the National Health Service at Wells Cathedral, 1998. Left to right: Pamela Williams, Joe Hull, Kim Rew, David Leonard, Sarah Matravers, Nigel Cavey, Carol Warren, Bruce Young, Natalie Williams, Derek Hobbs, Vera Metters, Rosemary Pester.*

❧ *Second World War and After* ❧

Stogumber Home Guard, 1942. Left to right, policemen on steps: SS G. Bryant, SC S. Dennett, SC J. Bryant; back row: L. Hyett, ?, A. Gulliford, J. Hutchings, S. Bennett, L. Chidgey, E. Stevens, J. Date, ?, W. Yeandle, SC N. Red, J. Hill, T. Stevens, B. Davis; front: J. Hayes, G. Fevre, Revd Ambrose Couch, Mrs H. Blatherwick, Miss Pam Maddock (kneeling), Mrs B. Mardon, F. Baker, Dr Atkinson, Col Hutchison, C. Thomas, J. Brewer, W. Hill.

Stogumber and District Home Guard, 1942.

Above: *Women's Land Army in front of their hostel (now Springfield Maltings) at the Old Brewery, Stogumber, 1944. Included are: Barbara Henson, Kath Webber, Muriel Hutchings, Honor Hayes, Doreen Stevens, Hilda Dean, Dorothy Sherman, Mrs Cold, Betty Hayes, Vera Davey.*

Right: *Former members of the Land Army based at Stogumber attending a reunion at Springfield Maltings, c.1990. Left to right, back row: Honor Hayes, Dorothy Sherman, Dorothy May, Grace Maddock; front: May ('Johnny') Davey, Vera Davey, Stella Long, Muriel Hutchings, Kath Webber.*

Left: *Richard Denot* (left) *and friends at the 50th anniversary of VE Day at Stogumber, 1995.*

Above: *Celebrating the 50th anniversary of VE Day at Stogumber, 1995. Holding the Women's Land Army banner is Honor Hayes with grandson Stephen.*

VE Day at Oldway, 1945.

Above: *Stogumber Red Cross, c.1950. Left to right, back row: J. Payne, M. Tuckfield, ?, ?, N. Ford, Mrs Bale, ?, A. Hole, Q. Payne, ?, ?, ?, B. Somerfield; front: ?, K. Houlder, B. Pearce, ?, B. Mardon, ?, E. Capewell, Nurse Trundle, Mrs Greswell. Miss Betty Mardon had a long association with the British Red Cross Society and was awarded life membership in recognition of 30 years' service, as well as being made honorary vice-president of the county on her retirement.*

Above: *Stogumber Red Cross, 1949. Left to right, back row: J. Hutchings, J. Trebble, N. Ford, Mrs Hume; middle: Mrs Bale, Q. Payne, ?, B. Pearse, ?; front: ?, C. Thomas, B. Mardon, A. Howell, Mrs Greswell.*

Right: *A section of Stogumber Red Cross, 1948. Left to right, back row: Sheila Criddle, Iris Milton; front: Myrtle Parsons, Mrs Mardon, Betty Mardon, Julie Payne.*

❧ *Farming* ❧

Hall Farm, Stogumber, c.1980. It is thought that this farm, formerly Hall Place, stands on the site of the capital messuage of the medieval rectorial estate. The buildings included a dovecot by 1439, and the construction of a barn was ordered in 1506. The paddock containing the barn appears to have been taken out of the original churchyard and it is possible that the ground north of the western half of the barn may contain early burials. Hall Farm had a small estate of just over 21 acres in and around Stogumber village, with one detached field called Hartrow Wood Plot south-east of Preston. The present house has been two, perhaps three, cottages and is now a small farm and guest-house with the privilege of a gravelled path through the churchyard.

Right: *Meet of the West Somerset Foxhounds at Hall Farm, Stogumber, 1988.*

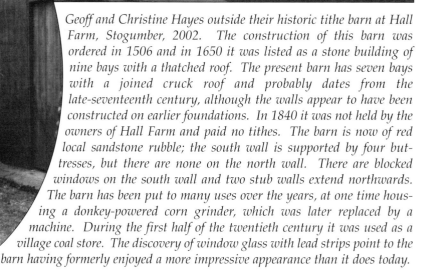

Geoff and Christine Hayes outside their historic tithe barn at Hall Farm, Stogumber, 2002. The construction of this barn was ordered in 1506 and in 1650 it was listed as a stone building of nine bays with a thatched roof. The present barn has seven bays with a joined cruck roof and probably dates from the late-seventeenth century, although the walls appear to have been constructed on earlier foundations. In 1840 it was not held by the owners of Hall Farm and paid no tithes. The barn is now of red local sandstone rubble; the south wall is supported by four buttresses, but there are none on the north wall. There are blocked windows on the south wall and two stub walls extend northwards. The barn has been put to many uses over the years, at one time housing a donkey-powered corn grinder, which was later replaced by a machine. During the first half of the twentieth century it was used as a village coal store. The discovery of window glass with lead strips point to the barn having formerly enjoyed a more impressive appearance than it does today.

Right: *Cruck beams supporting the roof of the seventeenth-century tithe barn at the farm.*

Far right: *The granary at Hall Farm, which dates back to the early 1800s.*

Combe Cross Farm (now Silverdown Cottage), c.1930s.

Above left: *Rowdon in 2002.*

Main and above: *Rowdon Farm, c.1930.*

Above: *Vivian Sellick holding the Perpetual Gold Cup which he won for the best Charolais female at the Royal Show, 1987.*

Above: *Roger Hutchings, who has lived at Stogumber all his life and farmed at Wood Farm.*

Above: *Pride of Escott Farm. Vivian Sellick* (right) *with Escott Rula and Geoffrey Sellick with her twin calves, winners of the prestigious Burke Trophy at the Royal Show in 1987. The bull belonged to a Mrs Ogden.*

Left: *HRH Prince Charles chatting with the vice-president of the Devon Cattle Breeders' Society at the Bath and West Show, 1977, accompanied by Geoffrey Sellick (president DCBS) and Mrs Sellick.*

Below: *Escott Farm, Stogumber, 1994.*

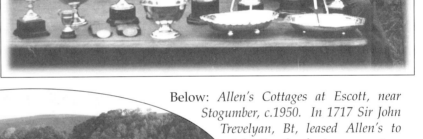

Below: *Mr H.E. Sellick, of Escott Farm, with some of the trophies won with his North Devon 'Red Ruby' cattle at various agricultural shows over a period of years.*

Above: *North Devon 'Red Ruby' bulls at Escott Farm, Stogumber, c.1950s.* Left to right: *Geoffrey Sellick, Bert Sellick, Alf Gratton.*

Below: *Charolais cattle grazing in a meadow at Escott Farm, 2002.*

Below: *Allen's Cottages at Escott, near Stogumber, c.1950. In 1717 Sir John Trevelyan, Bt, leased Allen's to John Routley for ten years at an annual rent of £16.*

Left: *Lower Preston Farmhouse, 2000.*

Below left: *Wood Farm, Stogumber, 1938.*

Below: *Harvesting spelt wheat at Lower Preston Farm, Stogumber, 1999. Driving the tractor is Paul ('Devon Boy') Kingdom.*

Harvest scene at Stogumber, c.1950s. **Left to right:** *Jack Hayes, Phyllis Bishop, Tom Besley, ?, Ted Stevens, George Bishop, ?, Geoff Hayes, Ron Hayes* **(holding son Michael),** *Honor Hayes with daughter Shirley.*

Haymaking at Vexford Farm is thirsty work!
Charlie Jones is second from the left, c.1920.

Right:
Harry Potter
with his two
tame
badgers at
Higher
Vexford,
c.1914.

Above: *Workers at*
Higher Vexford Farm,
c.1952. Left to right:
Brian and Bob
Somerfield, Ernest
Hoare, Jim Nation
senr, Adrian
Somerfield, Jim
Nation junr, Alfie
Gobles, Harry Webber.

Left: *Sheep shearing*
at Higher Vexford,
c.1900. George Potter
junr (left) and
shepherd George
Potter senr.

View of Stogumber from the top of Ling's Mead, c.1920.

Left: *Fat bullock in the Square, Stogumber, c.1910. Left to right: Stan Dennett, Basil Corney, Percy Hutchings.*

Bottom left: *Jim Criddle hand-milking cows at Hill Farm, c.1940.*

Below: *Stan Dennett at Hill Farm, Stogumber, c.1940.*

Above: *Capton House in the late-nineteenth century.*

Left: *Capton Sandstone Quarry, 2002.*

Below: *Curdon Mill, 2000.*

Left: *Haymaking at Stogumber, c.1940. Left to right, back: Hilda Deane, Jeff Criddle; middle: Jim Criddle, Land Army girl, Stan Dennett; front: Maurice Bryant.*

❧ *Vellow* ❧

Top: *Outside the forge at Vellow, c.1930s. Ernest Chilcott (blacksmith) and his wife Florence are on the far left and Eli Sawyer is third from the right.*

Above: *Outside the forge at Vellow, c.1920s. Left to right: Ern Chilcott, ?, Eli Sawyer, ?, ?, Fred Chilcott.*

Above right: *Ernest Chilcott outside the forge, c.1920s.*

Right: *Blacksmiths, c.1940s. Left to right: Jack Bryant, Bill Coles, Ern Chilcott.*

Above: *Vellow Wood, near Stogumber.*

Left: *David Winkley 'throwing' at Vellow Pottery, formerly the old forge.*

Vellow, c.1930s. The blacksmith's forge is last on the left.

❧ Cider! ❧

Right: *Albert Bartraham (left) and Carlo Criddle preparing the cider press.*

Below left: *Albert Bartraham (left) and Carlo Criddle pressing the cider 'cheese'.*

Below right: *Carlo Criddle enjoying a glass of locally-made cider in 1982. Carlo was one of Stogumber's characters and was a keen sportsman, playing both football and cricket for the village teams in his younger days.*

Left: *Albert Bartraham (left), Ann Williamson and Carlo Criddle enjoying the fruits of their labour.*

Above: *A badger dig at Stogumber, c.1900.*

Left: *After a successful Boxing Day's rabbiting at Stogumber, c.1930s.*

Below: *West Somerset Foxhounds at Hartrow Manor, c.1930s.*

❧ *Shops & Trade* ❧

Left: *Mrs P. Hutchings with three of her children (two looking out of the car roof) outside Gooding's shop, c.1920s.*

Below: *Blind basket-maker Bill Penny working at his craft, c.1955.*

Bottom right: *Christmas window display by butcher Percy Hutchings, c.1930s.*

Right: *Craftsman Leslie G. Bex busy in his workshop, c.1970. Lesley, a skilled woodworker, designed and made tableware and small pieces that were pleasing to the eye and much sought after. He would utilise to the fullest extent the beautiful grains, markings and colours of the Somerset timbers and finish simply with wax.*

Bottom left: *Gooding's shop staff at Stogumber, c.1950. Left to right: Jean Balman, Edna Criddle, Muriel Wilson.*

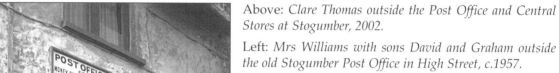

Inkpen's Stores at the Square, 1906.

Above: *Clare Thomas outside the Post Office and Central Stores at Stogumber, 2002.*

Left: *Mrs Williams with sons David and Graham outside the old Stogumber Post Office in High Street, c.1957.*

Above: *Enjoying a drink at the White Horse Inn, 1950. Left to right, back row: George Wise, Mrs Lillian Brewer (landlady), Tom Besley, Nicol Red; front: Bill Penny, Arthur Norman with Gill Brewer.*

Left: *The cabbage walking stick show at the White Horse Inn, Stogumber, 1993. Left to right: Terry Woodward, Ernie Wylie, Chris Comer, Ellen Williamson, Geoff Hayes, George Dyke.*

Above: *Stogumber Sports, c.1905.*

Right: *A group of Stogumber mothers, babies and toddlers, 1936. Left to right, back row: Mrs May Criddle with Sheila, Mrs Gladys Hawkins with Dick, Mrs Evelyn Dennett with Roy, Mrs Webber with baby, ?; front: Mrs Lewis with Reg, ?, ?, Audrey Jones, Robert Webber, Barbara Criddle.*

Left: *The Stogumber Christmas Party Committee, 1966. Left to right, back row: Hector Potter, Ron Penny, Arthur Bosley, Mary Bryant, Maurice Bryant; middle: Revd Paul Ashwin, Mrs G. Hawkins, Mrs Dennett, Mrs Criddle, Mrs Bosley, Mrs Hole, Mrs Alice Bryant, Sid Bryant; front: Harry Branchflower, Ernest Chilcott, Fred ('Daisy') Bryant, Mrs E. Hutchings.*

Below: *Playbus at Stogumber, 1980. Left to right, inside bus: Adrian Hill, Paul Jones, Graham Hill, Colin Jones, Janice Hayes holding Wayne Sawyer; others include: Joanne Hayes, Naomi Lewis, Debbie Garland, Anthony Cornish, Sharon Jones, Caroline Brayford, Elizabeth Brayford, Denise Brown, Michelle Jenkins, Bill Brayford, Daniel Winkley, Julia Hill holding Jason Comer, Paulette Hayes, Philip Ash, Christine Hayes, Andrew Jenkins and Tracey Thomas.*

Above: *Social gathering at Deane Close, Stogumber, c.1970. Left to right: Mrs Penny, Mrs D. Lock, Mrs Bellringer, Mrs Edith Criddle, Mrs G. Criddle.*

Stogumber Village Hall was originally known as the Church House, the first turf on the site being cut in May 1929 by the then vicar, the Revd Ambrose Couch, whose brainchild it was. Mr W.H. Pollard, of Bridgwater, was the builder, and electricity was installed by Messrs Sully & Sons, of Stogumber. Its total cost was £1,056.18s.9d., which included the additional sum of £50 for the provision of a good dance floor. It was opened in December that year by Mrs Mitchell. The dance floor was polished for hours and dressed with white talc and was the pride and joy of the vicar Ambrose Couch. When people arrived for a dance he would inspect their shoes and if they were not wearing appropriate dancing attire they would have to borrow one of the 50 spare pairs which he kept. Later called the Church Hall, one of the local social highlights was the annual dance held there in aid of Taunton Hospital. By 1960, as it became subject to District Council regulations, the building was becoming known as the Village Hall. The Village Hut was demolished in 1990 and £2,000 of funds belonging to it were transferred to the Village Hall. An extension consisting of a games room, kitchen, toilets and entrance lobby was begun in 1992 and completed the following year at a total cost of £47,810, extra costs being incurred due to subsidence at the southern end. Fund-raising efforts and a grant ensured that this was paid on time. The hall was reopened on 1 May 1993 by Mrs Eileen Zoers, director of the Community Council for Somerset, and by Mr Sandy Illingworth, chairman of the Hall Committee. Further improvements have since been made, and the first event at the newly-refurbished hall was the 2002 Stogumber Show.

Above: *British Legion church parade at Stogumber, 1929.*

Above: *Scouts visit Buckingham Palace, 1946. Left to right: John Hole, Roy Dennett, Viv Brewer, Dick Hawkins, Mostyn Brown, Tony Bryant.*

Right: *Cubs at Preston Vale, c.1946. Left to right: Tom Hawkins, Jim Dennett, Sid Hole, Clive Brewer (obscured), Dick Tremlett.*

Women's Institute

Stogumber WI, c.1949. Left to right, back row: *Mrs Horn, Mrs Duddridge, C. Hayes, B. Brewer, Mrs Nation, Mrs Red, ?, Nan Watts, Mrs Williams, Miss Stevens, E. Stevens, M. Clark, Miss Duddridge, Mrs Thorne, Mrs Tremlett, B. Williams, Mrs Wyatt, Mrs Lewis, Mrs Branchflower, Mrs Hole, Mrs Bex;* sitting: *Mrs Luhman, Mrs Hare, Mrs Somerfield, Mrs Allen, Miss Thomas, Miss Pearce, ?, ?, ?, Mrs Pharye, G. Hole, Mrs Bryant, A. Holder, Lady Holder, Mrs Austin, Miss Mardon;* sitting at table: *Mrs Freeman (president) with American guest.*

A WI was first founded at Stogumber in 1924, but unfortunately was closed in 1985. However, an open meeting was held in September 2000 to explore the possibility of re-forming a WI. This was followed by a further open meeting in November 2000 when the formation of a new Institute was confirmed. It now has over 20 enthusiastic members and plays an active part in village events. This photograph shows Stogumber WI, 2001. Left to right, back row: *Dr Ruth Wallace, Heather Bowring, Diana Axford, Heather Cosens, Mary Jenkins, Tricia Vandenheede, Elaine Leech, Judy Campbell, Monica Greenway, Jill Young;* front: *Margaret Dring, Margery Young, Audrey Leitch, Kate Ryder, Mary Field, Marjorie Bell, Glen Heaton, Daphne Faithorne, Mrs Sweeney.*

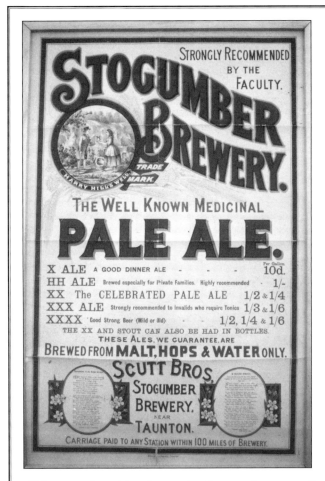

Stay, reader! Stay a little while,
Whilst fifty thou canst scarcely number,
And read, portray'd in homely style,
The praise and virtues of Stogumber.

Go search the Kingdom thro' and thro'
From Royal Thames to Northern Humber,
No ale, or porter, man can brew
Will bear the prize from bright Stogumber.

Ye cider sellers, hide your head;
Rejoice each painter and each plumber,
You all who dabble much in lead,
May safely quaff the pure Stogumber.

Does pain of mind, or pain of body,
Weigh you down and banish slumber?
Fly from brandy, gin or toddy,
But take a glass of rich Stogumber.

Do aching thighs (whene'er you move),
And stiffening joints your walk encumber?
Would you move brisk? Then haste and prove
The strengthening power of pure Stogumber.

But one month since, my legs were lank,
Each rib with ease I then could number:
But now I'm plump, and how? I drank
Each day, a pint of pale Stogumber.

Old poster advertising Stogumber Brewery beverages displayed at the White Horse Inn and an 1850 testimonial to Stogumber ale in verse.

STOGUMBER MEDICINAL ALE, so highly recommended by the Faculty, brewed with the water from HARRY HILL'S WELL, is now in prime condition, to be had in small casks as follow:—

		£	s	d
Treble X ... ... per Kilderkin ...	£1	7	0
Do. ... ... „ Firkin	0	14	0
Double X ... ... „ Kilderkin ...	1	3	0
Do. ... ... „ Firkin	0	12	0
Single X ... ... „ Kilderkin ...	0	18	0
Do. ... ... „ Firkin	0	9	0
Good Table Ales „ Kilderkin ...	0	15	0
Do. do. „ Firkin	0	7	6

Strong Old Beer, 18d. and 15d. per Gallon.

Orders received by letter or otherwise will have prompt attention.

H. WATTS, *Manager,*

Stogumber Brewery, Taunton.

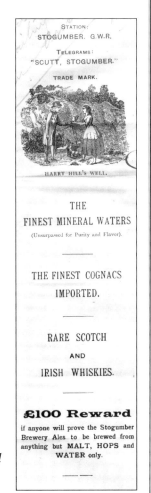

STATION:
STOGUMBER. G.W.R.

TELEGRAMS:
"SCUTT, STOGUMBER."

TRADE MARK.

HARRY HILL'S WELL.

THE
FINEST MINERAL WATERS
(Unsurpassed for Purity and Flavor).

——

THE FINEST COGNACS
IMPORTED.

——

RARE SCOTCH
AND
IRISH WHISKIES.

——

£100 Reward
if anyone will prove the Stogumber
Brewery Ales to be brewed from
anything but MALT, HOPS and
WATER only.

Advertisement for the brewery printed in the West Somerset Free Press *in 1872 and (right) a section from the brewery's headed paper, 1889.*

The Old Brewery, Stogumber. Before demolition the Brewery cellars were used, amongst other things, as a rifle range.

Stogumber Brewery

Charles George Elers founded Stogumber Brewery in 1840, water being used from Harry Hill's well, which was reputed to possess medicinal substances. In 1861 the brewery was owned by Major John Sloman, and in 1884, with Christmas approaching, it was offering ale at 10d.–1s.3d. a gallon, stout or porter at 1s.3d. a gallon, and beer at 1s.3d.–1s.6d. a gallon. Direct deliveries were made to consumers within a 15-mile radius. In an advertisement it was claimed that the ale would cure anything from leprosy to flatulence and that it was 'good for the clergy and others with weak lungs.'

In 1891 the brewery was sold for £1,650, but continued brewing ale into the twentieth century. Difficulties on the roads were encountered by the horse-drawn drays during the latter years of the nineteenth century, this being particularly the case down Shute Street and over the ford, which was at that time the continuation of Station Road and little more than a rough track.

The Brewery was run by the brothers Ernest and George Scutt in 1894, with the ale brewed solely from malt, hops and the medicinal waters of Harry Hill's well – which by this time were being strongly recommended to invalids as 'renovating and delicious'.

Several minerals and aerated waters were also manufactured by Scutts, using the celebrated waters. Their old mineral-water bottles are still found from time to time. Matthew Mossman was the brewer at Springfield in 1906, where employees were given a half-gallon jar of ale daily; it was claimed they thrived so well on it that few of them ever died before they were 80!

Brewing was discontinued in 1912, when the house became a private residence. In 1939 it was purchased by Major and Mrs May and soon afterwards was commandeered for the Women's Land Army. Springfield Maltings is today again a private residence, but the Old Brewery buildings have disappeared and Harry Hill's well is now overgrown and sadly neglected. Old Stogumber Brewery bottles *(right)* are still found in the parish hedgerows from time to time.

Mrs Jennings and her family about to set off on an outing in Joel Sully's 12/14hp Mitallurgique car, c.1912.

Above: *Outside Wick House, Stogumber, c.1930s.* Left to right, standing: *Frank Sully, Joel Sully;* sitting: *Sarah Sully.*

Right: *Sully staff outing to Lynmouth, c.1930s.* Left to right: *Joel Sully, Bill Brewer, Ethel Sully, John Allen, Mrs Allen, Owen Allen, Mrs Branchflower, Mr Branchflower.*

Below: *Joel Sully's riverside workshop* (left).

Below: *Lauriston House (former home of Joel Sully), Stogumber, 1917.*

Frank and Marjorie Sully outside the shop of the Misses Sully next to Wick House at Stogumber, c.1920s.

Joel Sully at the wheel of his Studebaker Light 6 car, 1914. In the back are his wife Ethel and son Frank. Mr Sully was the first villager to own a motor car.

A receipt from 1914.

Let There be Light

Stogumber was one of the first villages in West Somerset, and indeed amongst the earliest in the country, to have an electricity supply. It was here, in 1924, that garage proprietor Ernest Joel Sully, of his own initiative, translated 'new lamps for old' into practical terms and signalled the beginning of the end of the oil-lit age. Having received promises from a number of residents that they would 'take the light', he set about providing it, and the enterprise duly came to fruition with a public switching-on ceremony, performed by Mr Tom White, of Escott, in February 1924.

Mr White had previously urged Mr Sully to write to HRH The Prince of Wales (later to become King Edward VIII) inviting him to open Stogumber's electricity supply. This Mr Sully did, and received a letter in reply regretting that the Prince was unable to do so due to a prior engagement. Mr Sully's power station was his own riverside premises, and his plant was said to be capable of meeting all the needs of the village. Power was obtained with a 10/12hp Petters engine, Newton's, of Taunton, supplied a dynamo, and there was a 380amp battery. By the time of the switching-on ceremony about a dozen houses had been wired for electricity, as well as the Baptist Chapel nearby. Installations were made at the rate of £1 per light and a charge of 1s. per unit for the current.

On a dark February night Mr Tom White pulled a switch; Mr Sully's premises were brilliantly illuminated by coloured bulbs (the district's first 'fairy lights'?) and Stogumber shot several years ahead of most other villages in the district. Many people stood around to see the new marvel and optimistically envisaged a Stogumber with a few street lights!

Mr Sully was quite an entrepreneur, his other enterprises including building, undertaking and running a garage; he was also the owner of the first motor car in the village.

❧ Making Music ❧

Left: *Talented young Stogumber musicians, 1999. Left to right: Natalie, Emily, Stephanie and Timothy Cavey. Emily is the eldest of the four musically talented children of Nigel and Wendy Cavey, of Stogumber; she started playing the cello at the age of nine and gained a place with the National Children's Orchestra in her first year, remaining with them for four years, and within two years she gained a scholarship to Wells Cathedral School. For three consecutive years Emily was a member of the National Youth Orchestra of Great Britain and, having won a scholarship, is continuing her studies at the Royal Academy of Music at the time of writing. Twin sisters Natalie and Stephanie have both been learning the violin since the age of seven and, like their elder sister, were awarded special music scholarships to Wells Cathedral School to study violin and viola. Both were members of the National Children's Orchestra for five years and in 2003 are playing with the National Youth Orchestra of Great Britain, Stephanie with the first violins. Natalie and Stephanie were regional finalists in the BBC Young Musician of the Year competition in 2002. Timothy, the youngest of the four, attended Stogumber First School until the age of nine, when he also obtained a special music scholarship to Wells Cathedral School, where he studies the double-bass. He was a member of the National Children's Orchestra for three years and has won numerous first prizes as a soloist in the Taunton and Mid-Somerset Music Festivals. Tim has also met with success when playing in his family's wind and string ensembles and is an accomplished drum-kit player. A keen sportsman, he represents his school in all its team sports, and is a member of the Junior Somerset County Cricket Club.*

Above left: *A 'Sixpenny Hop' in the late 1940s. Left to right: Arthur Bosley, Sid Bryant, Joan Chorley.*

Above: *Roy Hyett's Dance Band, c.1930s. Left to right: John Furneaux, Arthur Bosley, Joe Buncombe, Roy Hyett.*

Left: *Halsway Manor House and Mews, beneath the Quantocks, is owned by the Halsway Manor Society and is home to Britain's only permanent residential folk-music centre. The manor dates from before 1066, but the house was rebuilt in the 1400s with further redevelopment in the late 1800s. Additions of panelling and plasterwork from old houses and other alterations were made in the early 1920s.*

Local Personalities

The late Percy Hutchings: Percy Hutchings was one of twins (boy and girl) and was among the best-known characters in the district, around which he used to trundle in his veteran car. He spent his entire life in West Somerset, being the younger son of the late Mr F. Hutchings, a family butcher at Bridge Street, Williton, and, like his brother, the late Mr Alfred Hutchings, Percy followed this trade. In 1909 he set up at Stogumber to become one of the many tradesmen in the days when the village was entirely self-supporting in this respect. He leased premises from the White Horse Inn, and his weekly outgoings, including full board for five days, rent and a boy's wages, were just 17s.6d. Later Percy married Ellen James and they lived in Stogumber, where their seven children were born.

In 1939 he acquired Williton Meat Supply, which was later taken over by his eldest son, Mr F.J. Hutchings. Percy was a Ministry grader for many years, and it is doubtful if anyone had a keener eye for a beast. He acted as judge at many Christmas fatstock shows, including Taunton, Barnstaple, Bridgwater, Wiveliscombe and Bampton. He also served as one of Stogumber's representatives on the old Williton Rural District Council from 1946 until 1955, and often provided a spark during debate.

Always interested in music, he was a clever pianist in his youth, and his services were in demand at the dances and entertainments at the big houses. He also played the organ and, in addition to officiating at the Parish Church at Stogumber, he was often to be found at the console in many other local churches, playing for weddings and funerals. He did this readily at the request of old friends.

An old footballer and cricketer, Percy had some outstanding contemporaries at both games. He was noted for his prowess as a dribbler on the football field, and in his cricket days at Stogumber he was often in the team with J.C. White, who was to go on to Somerset and England fame. Percy died in 1967, aged 86.

The late Leslie Hyett: Leslie Hyett was born at Stogumber in 1908 and during his long life he contributed in many ways to the village he loved, along with his father Seymour and sister Phyllis. Leslie organised the annual Taunton Hospital fancy-dress dance, which was one of the village's social highlights of the year and always packed the Church Hall. He was a supporter and regular player with the Cricket Club, and was secretary of the local Rifle Club and a keen shot. All his family were enthusiastic gardeners, helping to organise the local flower show, Leslie himself being a particularly gifted

grower of sweet peas. The family also ran the Christmas Tree Party for all the parish children, at which every school leaver received a Bible. Leslie helped with the blanket fund, through which families were given a blanket every third year, and he was a hard-working supporter of the Village Hut. Following his father into the trade as a plumber and builder, Leslie knew every individual, as well as every pipe and drain, in the village. He would turn out to help at any hour, day or night. As chairman of the Parish Council for 17 years, he is remembered for his wise counsel and for getting much done in a quiet and dignified manner. He will also be remembered for his daily habit of looking towards the church to see which way the weathercock was facing. Leslie was well versed in wildlife and an enthusiast in all country pursuits. He died in May 2001.

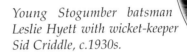

Young Stogumber batsman Leslie Hyett with wicket-keeper Sid Criddle, c.1930s.

The late Geoffrey Sellick: Geoffrey Sellick was born at Wiveliscombe, being the only child of Bert and Florrie Sellick. Geoff's parents moved to Chidgley when he was just three years old, his education beginning at Nettlecombe and continuing at Wellington School. Towards the latter part of his schooling Geoff's family moved to Escott Farm, Stogumber. Leaving school in 1943, Geoff worked on the family farm, taking over its running at the age of 18 when his father fell ill. In 1948 he married Kathleen Pile, from Bampton, Devon, who was born on a farm at Barbrook, North Devon, but left there at the age of two. The couple had two sons, Ken and Vivian, who carry on the family farming tradition.

In the 1950s, when the Nettlecombe estate was broken up, the family bought Escott Farm, and over the years the business grew as they acquired adjoining land. Hele and Battins Farms at Brompton Ralph were also purchased and are now amalgamated into one concern. In the early years at Escott the family built up one of the best herds of pedigree Red North Devon cattle ('Red Rubies'), and Geoff took great pride in showing these at both local and national events. In 1976 he founded the Escott herd of pedigree Charolais cattle, which is now known both nationally and internationally. Again he took enormous pride in showing these animals all around the country, and his proudest moment was winning, with his son Viv, the Burke Trophy (the inter-breed championship, the highest and most prestigious award in the country, and possibly the world, for

Above: *'Granny' Mullins with her six daughters, c.1950s. Left to right: Nessie Ford, Marjorie Pearcey, Norah Langsford, Agnes ('Granny') Mullins, Gladys Hewitt, Nellie Norton, Harriet Touchin.*

Right: *Agnes ('Granny') Mullins enjoying a day out at the seaside. Her family ran the bakery and shop at Stogumber for many years.*

Far left: *Gill Brewer astride Nicol Red's horse at Stogumber, 1953.*

Left: *Nurse Barbara Trundle, 1982. She has lived in the same house since her arrival in the village in 1950.*

Right: *Five gentlemen at Stogumber, c.1920s. Left to right: Mr Sweet-Escott, ?, Mr Joel Sully, Mr Charlie Howe, Mr Percy Duddridge.*

Left: *Vivian Brewer, Stogumber's representative on West Somerset District Council. At the time of writing he has so far served on the authority for 27 years, with two terms as chairman. Although now a resident of nearby Crowcombe, Viv spent much of his earlier years at Stogumber, where his father, William Brewer, ran a garage business and was a former landlord of the White Horse Inn.*

Geoffrey and Kathleen Sellick celebrate their golden wedding in 1998.

beef) at the Royal Show in 1987. His cattle were also exported to various countries.

Geoff was a leading member of Wiveliscombe YFC in his youth, was a long-serving member and past president of the Devon Cattle Breeders' Society, and was also on the committee of the National Beef Association. For three years he was president of the South West Charolais Association and a past president of Dunster Show as well as being a member for many years. He took a keen interest in most things happening around Stogumber, serving on the Parish Council for at least 45 years and acting as chairman for seven of them.

Geoff loved cricket and supported both the local and county clubs. He was also keen on skittles, playing with the same team at Crowcombe for 49 years. In 1991 Geoff retired from active farming and passed the business over to his sons. Both he and his wife took up a new sport – bowls – joining Williton Bowling Club and becoming very enthusiastic members. Geoff was a countryman through and through, he loved the countryside and everything in it and he was also a brilliant stockman. He died in May 2002, aged 76.

The late Bob Somerfield: Robert John (Bob) Somerfield was born at Chidgley, but spent most of his life in Stogumber. He worked on local farms, at first with horses, and excelled at all kinds of farm work. In 1935 he married Christabel Warren and they raised four children; Christabel died in 1981, a year before Bob's retirement.

Bob Somerfield, with daughter Barbara Vearncombe, after receiving Maundy Money from HM the Queen at Wells Cathedral in 1993.

Bob was a well-known bell-ringer, being a member of the Bath and Wells Diocesan Association of Change Ringers for over 40 years and a past ringing master and secretary of Dunster Deanery. He made many friends through bell-ringing at churches throughout the South West, and the family tradition of bell-ringing was carried on by succeeding generations. Bob was a churchwarden at Stogumber for over 20 years and was always willing to help anyone in need. In 1993, in recognition of his work for the church, he was chosen to receive Maundy Money from the Queen at Wells Cathedral – an honour of which he was very proud.

He also won great respect as area representative for the National Farm Workers Union. Bob died in May 1995, aged 81 years.

Right: *Three generations of Somerfield bell-ringers.* Left to right: *Adrian, Bob and Iain Somerfield.*

Left: *Hector and Daisy Tuckfield outside Buckingham Palace before the garden party, July 1998.*

The late Hector Tuckfield: Hector Tuckfield was born in Stogumber and, apart from when he saw active service during the Second World War, remained in the village all his life. He was a popular character and well-known member of the West Somerset community. One of four sons born to Mr and Mrs Reginald Tuckfield, he attended the village school, leaving at the age of 14.

He began work as an apprentice gardener at Willett House, where his lifelong love of gardening began to germinate. Hector then moved to the Nettlecombe estate. When war broke out in 1939, he joined the Royal Army Service Corps, where he rose to the rank of sergeant, eventually being made sergeant-major. He was in charge of a platoon involved in the Normandy landings on D-Day (6 June 1944), going ashore at Sword Beach. A few weeks later he was with the Americans on Omaha Beach and was later decorated with the USA's Bronze Star.

Hector returned to Stogumber after hostilities ceased and began work with the highways department of Williton Rural District Council. Ill-health forced him to retire at the age of 57.

He married Daisy Margaret May in 1940, and they had two children, Margaret and George. Hector's love of gardening was epitomised by his magnificent garden at Quantock View, where he lived with his family for many years. A keen sportsman, he played football for Stogumber, Watchet and Monksilver, played skittles for the White Horse Inn for a number of years and was an enthusiastic follower of local hunts.

However, cricket was his greatest sporting love, and he began playing for the village team in his early teens and for many years was club captain. Disappointed when the club moved to Williton in the 1970s, he was delighted when they returned to Stogumber at their new ground at the top of Station Hill. He became club vice-president and was a regular spectator at home matches.

Hector took an active part in the community life of the village. For 25 years he was a parish councillor and his local knowledge was often sought out. His dedication to the village was rewarded when he and Daisy were invited to a Royal Garden Party at Buckingham Palace in 1998. He died in 2000, aged 83.

George Tuckfield: George Tuckfield was brought up in Stogumber, being the son of well-known village residents Daisy and the late Hector Tuckfield. Following his education, George became a reporter on the *West Somerset Free Press* where he received a good grounding under the watchful eye of the late Jack Hurley for his future career in journalism. After eight years with the *Free Press*, George moved to Maidenhead in Berkshire; at the time of writing he is the editor of the *Henley Standard* in South Oxfordshire. George often returns to Stogumber, where his mother still lives, and has kindly penned the following lines:

Growing up in Stogumber during the late 1940s and '50s was, simply, great fun. The war was over, sons of the village were returning from the battlefields, life was returning to normal. An ageing memory often plays tricks, but these were wonderful, carefree days still vividly etched in my mind.

My life at that time was a rollercoaster of fun, revolving around family, the church, school and sport. All too often these days you hear young people, particularly in a small village, I suppose, complaining that they have nothing to do. Well, we made our own fun. There were darker moments, of course. Kicking a football through a window in what used to be the doctor's surgery opposite the White Horse Inn meant a ticking off from village bobby P.C. Harris. I was a terrified four-year-old at the time. And then there was the slipper! We would go on school nature walks around the village fields and, on this particular occasion, a friend and I decided there was no point in returning to school in the afternoon. We reasoned that we would only arrive back in time to be sent home. The following morning we were summoned by headmistress Mrs Howe, who was, incidentally, a marvellous first teacher for any youngster. On this particular day, however, my thoughts were not quite so complimentary. My punishment was five slaps on each hand with her infamous slipper!

On the fun side it was cricket and football; another favourite was a ride on farmer Nicol Red's horse and cart, and who can forget those haunting ghost stories by the vicar, the Revd John Cox, at the Christmas parties held in the Village Hall? The church, of course, was an integral part of village life. For several years I was a member of the choir and this involved the obligatory choir practice on a Friday night. Well, Friday nights in the summer were also practice nights for the cricket

team, but the choir came first and then it was a quick dash to The Knap to watch the likes of Ern Hayes, Bert Sully, brothers Ron and Geoff Hayes, Bernard Williams, Geoffrey Sellick, Robin Bex, my dad Hector, my uncle Percy and others practising – but not before they had cleared up the cow pats in the outfield for the match the following day! Football was also played on The Knap in those days when the village team was certainly a force to be reckoned with. The club ceased in the early 1950s, but football was pretty popular with a few of us kids in the village and we managed to persuade Maurice Bryant to form a youth team which played in the West Somerset League in the late 1950s and into the '60s. Our ground was on the present cricket field, and I wonder what groundsman 'Taffy' Jenkins would say now if footballers with long-studded boots were running all over his beloved square?

Although I had by that time left for pastures new, it was a sad day when it was decided to close down the 'old' cricket club in the 1970s. I have some wonderful memories of the 'friendly' games we then played and the characters who played. Suffice to say, it was a true red-letter day when cricket returned to the village. Long may the 'new' club continue.

Also long may the recently-threatened White Horse pub, now under new management, continue. Stogumber without a pub and skittles on a Monday night? Perish the thought! Ah, happy memories!

Nurse Barbara Trundle: One of Stogumber's most respected and esteemed residents is Nurse Barbara Trundle, district nurse/midwife/health visitor. She qualified as a nurse before the Second World War and then enlisted in Queen Alexandra's Imperial Military Nursing Service. She became a theatre sister and later specialised as an ophthalmic theatre sister. In 1948 she left the Services, having served in Normandy and Burma during the conflict.

She obtained her midwifery qualifications and arrived in Stogumber, working with Drs Roy and Mary Meyers at the Manor House surgery. She started a playgroup in the village and also took keep-fit classes, both in the old Village Hut. Before retiring in 1974, Nurse Trundle delivered 250 babies in this area. Among her other accomplishments in the village, she was secretary and treasurer of the Village Hut, has been a bell-ringer and helped with the church cleaning and she also served as a parish councillor. In earlier times she was a keen photographer and cine-fan, taking several films of life in the area in the 1950s, '60s and '70s.

Following retirement, she was able to further indulge in her hobbies which, besides photography, included lapidary (cutting and polishing stones), calligraphy, needlework and gardening (for many years her garden was open to the public during the Stogumber open-gardens weekend). Nurse Trundle also took and obtained an Open University degree in geology – a truly caring and talented lady.

Stogumber Cricket Club

It was with considerable pride that the village of Stogumber welcomed many distinguished guests and visitors to celebrate the opening of the magnificent new cricket ground and pavilion in its panoramic setting at Station Road on Saturday 13 May 1995. The opening was performed by former Somerset batsman Dennis R.W. Silk, CBE, JP, past president of the MCC and chairman at that time of the Test and County Cricket Board. Mr Silk also presented scrolls to life member George Dyke and fellow trustees of the club Sandy Illingworth, Graham Sherren, John Greswell and John Eddows, who were all made life members. Mr Roger Knight, secretary of the MCC, Sir Tim Rice and Tom King, MP, were amongst the guests.

The day marked the culmination of five years' hard work by a dedicated group of cricket lovers who freely gave of their time and resources to create and construct a truly marvellous ground and pavilion – without doubt one of the best in West Somerset. The ground itself was previously a hard-grazed field. Stogumber Cricket Club was founded in about 1875 and it appears that the club used various fields and grounds, the most well known being The Knap. In the mid-1970s support dwindled and The Knap went under the plough. Stogumber's most famous player was J.C. (Jack) White, who went on to play for and captain Somerset and England; another player, W.T. Greswell, also played for Somerset. Among other well-known local names to represent the club over the years were Hyett, Tuckfield, Hayes, Sansom, Criddle, Bryant, Gooding, Horsey, Hutchings, Hawkins, Williams, Penny, Brewer and Bex, the club being especially well served by Seymour Hyett, Hector Tuckfield and Ron Hayes.

In 1985 a few stalwart lovers of cricket met with the idea of bringing the game back to Stogumber. There was no ground to play on and, most important of all, there was no money. With enthusiasm and determination the club was reborn and funds were raised. For four years matches were played at Crowcombe and Williton. The club joined the West Somerset League in 1988, were promoted from the fourth to the third division in their first year and completed a successful season in Division 1 in 2003. The Nuclear Electric Knockout Cup was won by the club in 1991 and 1993.

In 1990 it was decided that the club should have its own ground. A piece of grazing land on the outskirts of the village was purchased and so began a remarkable transformation. In five years it was turned into one of the finest and most picturesque village cricket grounds in Somerset, with fine strips on the square being prepared by groundsman 'Taffy' Jenkins. The club runs two teams and improvements and additions are continually being made to the ground and pavilion. The venue and facilities are much sought after by touring teams and are used on occasions for county testimonial matches.

The night before the opening of the ground in 1995, Mr Sherren and his wife Judy, together with club president John Stace and his wife Ros, entertained the guests, trustees, club chairman Darby Ash, vice-chairman, treasurer and captain Cliff Matravers to dinner at Hartrow Manor. On the great day itself an entertaining game followed the ceremony, with distinguished personalities and former England and county players participating.

Stogumber Cricket Club, 1913. **Left to right, back row:** *Reg Tuckfield, Revd Ambrose Couch, P. Hutchings, W. Hyett, T. Sparks, T.L. White, Lyddon Cornish, W.T. Greswell, Comer White;* **front:** *Jack Tuckfield, Fred White, J.C. White (later captain of Somerset and England), Seymour Hyett, George Sansom.*

Left: *Stogumber Cricket Club, c.1936. Left to right, back row: Jim Sansom, Les Hyett, Ern Hayes, Reg Braunton, Lyddon Cornish, Harold Bryant, Bill Brewer, Ern Chilcott; front: Morley Sansom, Arthur Routley, Ron Gooding, ?, Jack Sansom.*

Right: *Stogumber Cricket Team, c.1970s. Left to right, back row: Andy Hayes, Robert Hutchings, Nick Sully, Alan Bulpin, Norman Barnes, Martin Scott; front: Edward Martin, Chris Polsom, Mike Hayes, Philip Watts.*

Left: *An old Stogumber XI in a cricket match in 1992 against the then Stogumber XI. Left to right, back row: Robin Bex, Robert Hayes, Andrew Hayes, David Armstrong, Michael Hayes, Vic Hayes, Philip Watts; front: Hector Tuckfield (umpire), Gary Church, George Tuckfield, Martin Scott, Keith Norcutt.*

Right: *Stogumber Cricket Club, Nuclear Electric Cup winners, 1993. Left to right, back row: D. Summerside, A. Jenkins, D. Bryant, Martin Hole, Mark Hole, K. Norcutt; front: M. Hayes, T. Auton, C. Matravers (captain), F. Penny, D. Jenkins.*

Left: *Stogumber Under-13 team, 1999, winners of the West Somerset Cricket League Under-13s Cup and the Knock-out Cup.* Left to right, back row: *Nick Sander-cock, Tim Auton (coach), Alex Appleby, Daniel Cawthorne, Chris Weetch;* front: *Stephen Hawkins, Oliver Rew, Daniel Barnes, Stephen Hayes, James Weetch.*

Above: *Stogumber Cricket Club 2nd XI, 2000.* Left to right, back row: *Jeremy Danson, Rod Price, Paul Weldon, David Gliddon, Jonathan Moorhouse;* front: *Steve Hayes, Mike Rawle, Keith Norcutt, Mostyn Symes, Daniel Barnes.*

Above: *Stogumber Cricket Club 1st XI, 2002.* Left to right, back row: *Phil Baker, Steve Hayes, Brian Penny, Tim Auton, Cliff Matravers, Garry Allington;* front: *David Bryant, Stuart Thorne, Jimmy Rexworthy, Simon Penny, Neil Lane.*

Above: *Stogumber Cricket Club trophy winners, 2002.* Left to right, back row: *Daniel Barnes, Nick Bennett, Steve Hayes, Jimmy Rexworthy, Jamie Robinson;* front: *Chris Weetch, James Weetch, Ian Ware.*

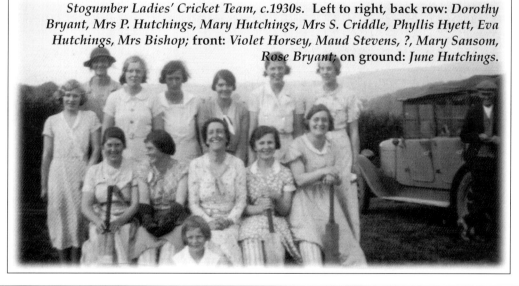

Stogumber Ladies' Cricket Team, c.1930s. Left to right, back row: Dorothy Bryant, Mrs P. Hutchings, Mary Hutchings, Mrs S. Criddle, Phyllis Hyett, Eva Hutchings, Mrs Bishop; front: Violet Horsey, Maud Stevens, ?, Mary Sansom, Rose Bryant; on ground: June Hutchings.

The pavilion at Stogumber cricket ground, 2002.

Above: *Darby Ash* (left) *and Sir Tim Rice tucking into the jam and cream scones during the tea interval at the game to celebrate the opening of Stogumber's magnificent new cricket ground and pavilion in Station Road. The match ended in a draw. The scores were: Dennis Silk's XI 262-8 dec. (R. Knight 73, B. Rose 44, V. Marks 39, T. King 31, D. Summerside 3-42). Stogumber 196-5 (C. Matravers 76, K. Norcutt 34, D. Bryant 32 n.o.).*

Right: *Hector Tuckfield* (left) *and Tom King (then the local MP) chatting at the opening of Stogumber's new cricket ground, 1995.*

Below: *Dennis Silk speaking at the opening ceremony of Stogumber Cricket Club's new ground and pavilion, 1995. Tom King (then the local MP) is on his right.*

Above: *Three generations of the Hayes family, whose 65-year association with Stogumber Cricket Club is still going strong. Left to right: Stephen, aged 16 and a member in 2003, Michael, Stephen's father, a player for 36 years, Ron, Stephen's grandfather, a player for 26 years and secretary for 13. Ron's brother Geoffrey was president of Stogumber Cricket Club at the time of his death in 2003.*

Stogumber groundsman D. ('Taffy') Jenkins, 2002.

JOHN CORNISH (JACK) WHITE is remembered as Stogumber's most famous cricketer. A son of Mr and Mrs T.L. White, of Escott Farm, he was a slow left-arm spin bowler of considerable guile and played for Somerset from 1909–37, being captain from 1927–31. He played 15 times for England, captaining them on four occasions. Touring Australia in 1928–9, he dismissed 25 men in the five Tests, helping England to win the Ashes. At Adelaide, in the fourth Test of the series, he bowled 124 overs and took 13 wickets for 256 runs in sweltering heat. To extol his performance 'Down Under', Taunton School published the following couplet in their magazine: 'Farmer White took fower for seven, all against Australia's crack eleven.' On White's return the young men of the village met him at Stogumber Station and triumphantly pulled him and his wife the two miles back to Escott on a farm wagon.

In 1921 at Worcester he took all ten wickets in an innings for 76 runs and four times took nine wickets in an innings. When Gloucestershire were dismissed for just 22 in their first innings in 1922 White took 7–10, but Somerset still lost the match by four wickets!

STEPHEN HAYES was born in 1986 and has the distinction of being the first Stogumber cricketer to represent the county at any level since J.C. (Jack) White. Through the county he played every year for the South West region in the Corners competition from the age of ten, and went on to represent Somerset in the Under-13s, -14s and -15s competitions. Stephen played for Stogumber Under-13s from the age of nine and captained them from 1996 through to 1999, when they won both the West Somerset Cricket League Under-13s Cup and the Knock-out Cup. He captained teams both at Danesfield School, Williton, and West Somerset Community College, leading Danesfield to their first ever victory in the State School Cup competition in 2000, and the Community College team to victory in the Somerset State Schools Cricket League in 2002. Stephen made his debut for a Stogumber men's team when he played in a 2nd XI game at the age of ten. Season 2002 was his first playing for Stogumber 1st XI, when he took 42 wickets, and it would be fitting if he went on to emulate former Stogumber players Jack White and Bill Greswell and gain a place in the county first team. Stephen comes from well-known local cricketing stock, his father Mike Hayes, grandfather Ron Hayes and uncle Andy Hayes all being former Stogumber players, whilst grandfather Reg Smith played for Watchet and great-grandfather John Hayes for Crowcombe. John and Ron Hayes and Reg Smith were all renowned big hitters of a cricket ball.

THE LATE GEOFFREY HAYES It is with deep regret that the authors pen this tribute to Geoffrey Hayes, of Hall Farm, and they are greatly indebted to him and his wife Christine for their help with parts of the Stogumber section of this book, the publication of which he was much looking forward to. Geoff, as he was known to all, was a Stogumber man through and through, and his outstanding contribution to the life of the village will be greatly missed. A local man described Geoff as 'the kindest man in Stogumber, who would do anyone a good turn if he could and would not hurt a fly.' Geoffrey Robert Hayes was born at Northam Mill, Stogumber, being the youngest of four. He attended Stogumber School and at the age of 14 began work at Escott Farm. In 1961 he married Christine Norman, of Hall Farm, and they had a son, Robert, and a daughter, Janice. He left Escott in 1962 to work at Hall Farm and continue a newspaper delivery business developed by Christine. A keen contributor to village life and supporter of events, Geoff joined Stogumber Church Choir as a boy and became its longest-standing member to date, being a chorister for over 65 years – choir practice and church services were very precious to him. He had been a school governor, a member of the PCC, a member of the CRASH committee, and a Village Hall trustee. Geoff could also be relied upon to be responsible for the erection of the Christmas tree in the Square and to help with the monthly village breakfast. Cricket was one of Geoff's great passions, and at the time of his death was president of Stogumber Cricket Club. He was also a keen supporter of the county club and could often be spotted with his brother Ron and friends in the Riverside Stand at the County Ground at Taunton. Skittles was another of Geoff's interests, and Tuesday evenings in winter would find him skittling with fellow farmers. Geoff was keenly interested in horticulture and spent much time in his garden, especially nearing the approach to the annual village flower show, in which he would enter exhibits and win certificates. He was very proud of his 'cabbage walking stick' plants and keen to share tips to produce the tallest; he enjoyed the friendly rivalry of the annual competition. Geoffrey Hayes died in June 2003, aged 73, and the esteem and regard in which he was held was reflected when over 300 family and friends packed the Parish Church for his funeral service.

❧ *Football* ❧

Stogumber Football Club, 1911–12. **Left to right, back row:** *?, J. Hayes, J. Tuckfield, ? Hall, ? Norman, Dr Ardagh, Ike Hole, S. Norman, J. Burge, P. Tuckfield, Bert Hole (trainer);* **front:** *G. Sansom, H. Burston, ?, Ted Stevens, J. Maddock, Reg Tuckfield.*

Right: The Football Club, 1913–14.

Below: Stogumber, cup winners, 1934–5. Left to right, back row (players only): *Carlo Criddle, Phil Langdon, Tom Gooding, Ern Hayes, Jim Sansom;* front: *Percy Watts, John Furneaux, Ted Stevens, Bill Horsey, Ron Gooding, Arthur ('Pump') Routley.*

Above: *Stogumber Football Club, Rosebowl winners, 1935–6.* Left to right, back row: *Arthur Gurney, Percy Watts, Albert Bartraham, S. Criddle, Carlo Criddle, Cliff Tremlett, ?;* middle: *Fred Grandfield, Ron Gooding, Ted Stevens, Arthur ('Pump') Routley, Bill Sully;* front: *Bill Horsey, ? Bartraham.*

Right: *Stogumber Football Club, 1947–8.* Left to right, back row: *J. Tuckfield, A. Gratton, C. Criddle, S. Gadd, S. Young (president), E. Hayes, J. Davey, T. Hole, A. Routley;* middle: *W. Brewer, J. Henson, G. Hutchings, C. Chilcott, S. Butler, M. Bryant, B. Box;* front: *R. Chilcott, H. Tuckfield, P. Tuckfield, L. Davey, J. Taylor, G. Webber.*

Left: *Stogumber Youth Football Club, 1958–9.* Left to right, back row: *M. Bryant (team manager), T. Lewis, A. Gimblett, W. Lee, B. Bradner, M. Lang, D. Coggins, T. Gratton;* front: *G. Tuckfield, J. McArten, M. Criddle, W. Williams, V. Hayes.*

Stogumber Football Club dinner at the Church Hall, c.1930s.
Left to right, back row: *A. Routley, Jim Sansom, T. Gooding, P. Watts, R. Gooding,*
E. Stevens, C. Criddle, E. Hayes, J. Furneaux, F. Hutchings, W. Horsey;
front: *Mrs Gurney, Dr Penberthy, L. Cornish, T.L. White, A. Gurney, Col Hutchison, G. Sadler.*

Stogumber Football Club dinner at the Church Hall, 1947.

| ❧ *Skittles* ❧ |

Above: *White Horse Inn skittles team, 1956.* Left to right, back row: *John Ribbons, Christine Kibblewhite (landlady), Geoff Hayes, Fred Sully, Bernard Kibblewhite (landlord), George Tuckfield, Ron Hayes;* front: *Hector Tuckfield, Bert Sully, Charlie May, Sam Gadd.*

Left: *Stogumber skittles team, White Horse Stallions, 2003.* Left to right, back row: *N. Bennett, D. Harris, R. Harris, D. Jenkins;* middle: *Martin Scott, Simon Penny, Andrew Jenkins;* front: *Chris Weetch.*

Below: *Enjoying skittles at King George V's Silver Jubilee celebrations at Stogumber in 1935.* Left to right: *Frank Hayes, Jim Horsey, Spencer Lyddon, Harry Branchflower, Seymour Hyett.*

Some of Pop's Boys skittles team from Stogumber after receiving their awards at a presentation evening in the early 1970s. Left to right: *David Williams, Frank Penny, Martin Scott, David Bartraham.*

Coronation Celebrations, 1953

A large programme of sports for adults and children was one of the main features of Stogumber's celebrations at the Coronation of Queen Elizabeth II on Tuesday 2 June 1953, although inclement weather in the afternoon made it necessary for a slight postponement. The bells of St Mary's Church, which were rung frequently throughout the day, heralded a festive occasion. Arrangements were made by a committee comprising Messrs E. Chilcott (chairman), E.S. Nation (secretary and treasurer), F. Bryant, L. Hyett, C. Duddridge and E. Scott, and Mesdames C. Brewer, P. Hutchings, Horn, Freeland, C.V. May, H. Somerfield and G. Rawle. The church bell-ringers were Messrs A. Routley, S. Bryant, P. Tuckfield, R. Bex, R. Hawkins, P. Watts, J. Hawkins, B. Somerfield, W. Yandle, R. Dennett, B. Ridler and S. Dennett.

The vicar, the Revd W.J.P. Cox, and Pastor J. Sidwick (the Baptist minister) conducted an open-air service as the first part of the celebrations in Ling's Mead. Mrs P. Hutchings was the convenor for a tea provided in two sittings for the whole parish, and she was assisted by other ladies of the committee and helpers. Prior to the sports, children received souvenir Coronation mugs at the hands of the Misses S. and L. Sully. In addition, a kind gesture by Mr F. Beadle of Willett found each child in the parish in possession of a 2s.6d. savings stamp. Mrs E.S. Nation made this presentation.

For a lengthy sports programme, Mr Seymour Hyett, Major C.V. May and Mr E.H. Scott acted as judges. Mr G. Rawle (starter) and Messrs E. Chilcott,

F. Bryant, C. Duddridge and L. Hyett (stewards) were principally concerned with the arrangements.

Music by loudspeaker was provided in Ling's Mead during the day's activities, the equipment being supplied by Mr C.W. Ireland (Porlock). Mr H. Court was in charge of these arrangements, while the sale of ice-cream was supervised by Mrs L. Bex. Mr H. Branchflower and members of the local branch of the British Legion were in charge of a skittles competition. The day drew to a successful conclusion with a social, music being supplied by an amplifier, and dancing and games were conducted by Mr R. Bex. Refreshments were served by Mesdames Hawkins, Bryant, Dennett and Bex. Winners of the skittles competition were: ladies, 1st Mrs R. Hayes, 2nd Miss C. Norman, 3rd Mrs A. Balman; gentlemen, 1st W. Chidgey, 2nd C. Criddle, 3rd R. Hayes.

The sports results (in 1st, 2nd, 3rd order) were as follows: flat race, girls under 7, J. Bryant, J. Bryant, ? Kennedy; ditto, boys, B. Davey, F. Sully, M. Partington; girls under 9, R. Watts, W. Bailey, D. Lewis; ditto, boys, J. Hayes, J. Nation, A. Somerfield; girls under 11, R. Watts, M. Bailey, R. Hyett; ditto, boys, P. Maddon, J. Hay, R. Williams; girls under 14, J. Light, A. Gratton, D. Paver; ditto, boys, W. Chidgey, V. Hayes, G. Bryant; three-legged race, boys, G. Tuckfield and R. Williams, W. Hayes and G. Bryant, M. Criddle and W. Chidgey; sack race, boys, W. Chidgey, G. Bryant, T. Gratton; egg-and-spoon race, girls, D. Paver, M. Walford, J. Criddle; relay race, boys, H. Hill, T. Gratton, M. Criddle; ditto, girls, J. Criddle, J. Light, J. Duddridge; marathon race, J. Nation, T. Hole, C. Brewer (4th T. Bryant); flat race, ladies, J. Criddle, W. Pavey, P. Hole; ditto, men, L. Davey, W. Bryant, C. Brewer; obstacle race, boys under 4, M. Bailey, R. Williams, G. Bryant; egg-and-spoon race, ladies, W. Pavey, P. Hole, Mrs Clarke; thread-the-needle race, Miss M. Walford, Mr R. Hayes, Miss C. Norman; obstacle race, men, T. Tremlett, H. Hill, P. Allen; sack race, ladies, Miss Pavey, Miss C. Norman, Miss M. Walford; over 60s race, men, Mr May, F. Bryant, M. Nation; sack race, men, S. Hole, J. Potter, P. Allen.

Left: *Street party at Slade Close, Stogumber, to celebrate the Queen's Silver Jubilee, 1977.*

❧ *Royal Celebrations* ❧

Background image: *Celebrating the Queen's Golden Jubilee at Sawpits Close, Stogumber, 2002.*

Left: *Happy group at Stogumber in celebration of the Queen's Golden Jubilee, 2002.* Left to right: *Sandy and Joe Hull, Alf West* (hidden)*, Clare, Edward, Chris and Sophie Thomas.*

Right: *Pte Ron Penny, of Stogumber, who was honoured to form part of the Queen's Coronation Parade Detachment from REME, 1953.*

❧ Plays & Pageants ❧

Above: *Stogumber Pageant, 1931. This pageant-play, based on the history of the parish 1212–1689, was produced to help clear off the remaining debt on the Church Hall. It was entirely a local effort, written and staged by the Revd Ambrose Couch (vicar), and the whole of the scenery was planned and painted by Mr G.P. Fevre, headmaster of the village school. Three performances were given in January and it was performed again with two shows in December the same year.*

Above: *Part of the cast of Stogumber Pageant, 1931. Left to right: ?, R. Tuckfield, ? Bryant, Joel Sully, St John Couch, Revd Ambrose Couch, Ethel Sully, P. Watts, ?, P. Hutchings.*

Left: *Play performed at Stogumber Church Hall, c.1950. Left to right, back row: Sheila Tuckfield, Barbara Jewell, Sid Bryant, Margaret Gavin, Geoff Hayes, Pam Penny; front: Tom Besley, Ron Penny.*

Village Dances

Above: *Annual dance at Stogumber Church Hall in aid of Taunton Hospital, c.1930.*

Right: *Mistletoe Dance at the Church Hall, 1950.*

Left: *Princess Dance at the Regal Ballroom, Minehead, c.1958. Sitting centre are Margaret Tuckfield* (left) *and Linda Gadd.*

Right: *Group at a Carnival Princess Dance at Stogumber, c.1947.* Left to right, back row: *Joyce Hill, Violet Horsey, Hilda Criddle, Peggy Thomas, Vera Bryant, Pamela Hole;* front: *Iris Taylor, Barbara Criddle, Pamela Maddock, Margaret Routley, Vera Taylor.*

❧ Musical Events ❧

Right: *Trio performing at a Stogumber concert, 1948. Left to right: Sheila Criddle, Myrtle Parsons, Ann Bex.*

Below: *Concert party at Stogumber, 1948. Left to right, back row: Pam Penny, Geoff Hayes, Percy Tuckfield, Tom Besley, Jack Norton, Barbara Criddle; front: Lesley Bex, Ron Penny, Margaret Gavin, Sid Bryant, Ann Bex, John Hole, Sheila Smith.*

Left: *Entertainment at Stogumber Village Hall to raise funds for the local music festival, 1992. Left to right: Carol Warren, Joe Hull, Les Simms, Vera Metters, David Leonard, Gilly Tatlow.*

Right: *Stogumber Handbell Ringers performing in Chapel Arts, 2003. Left to right: Elizabeth Blazey, Mary Field, Bethan Harvey-Bishop, Jenny Hibbert, Mary Green, Bruce Young.*

❧ *Festivals & Fêtes* ❧

Left: *Stogumber School celebrating a 'Maying' Festival with the crowning of a May Queen and floral procession, 1962. Joan Podberry (seated, centre) is the May Queen and among her attendants are Sheila Criddle and Wendy Penny.*

Below: *Maypole dancing at Stogumber School, 1994.*

Background image: *Crowd at the 1982 Stogumber Festival.*

Below: *Ladies' tug-of-war at Stogumber Fete, 1999. Left to right: Mandy Speers, Emma Speers, Lorraine Shopland, Leanne Barnes, Carron Scott, Michelle Harris.*

Below: *Stogumber Festival poster, 1982.*

TAUNTON CIDER STOGUMBER FESTIVAL

TUESDAY 10th to SUNDAY 15th AUGUST 1982
To be opened by Lieutenant Commander Francis D. Drake MVO RNR
on Tuesday 10th August at 2.30 p.m.

Saxon to 20th Century
Costume Pageant in Parish Church

FESTIVAL OF FLOWERS
MUSICAL CONCERTS • POETRY READINGS
MUSEUM & EXHIBITIONS
ART, CRAFT AND PRODUCE STALLS
ROLLS ROYCE STATIC DISPLAY

PRESENTATION OF PRIZES IN VILLAGE SQUARE
BY THE TAUNTON CIDER WASSAIL QUEEN AT 4.00 P.M. ON
SATURDAY 14th AUGUST. PROCEEDS TO
STOGUMBER CHURCH FUND.

TAUNTON CIDER

Right: *Four Stogumber Festival 'likely lads', 1982!* **Left to right, back:** *Geoff Hayes, Dick Hawkins, Roy Dennett;* **front:** *Robin Bex.*

❋ Village Shows ❋

Right: *It's a Knock-out at Stogumber, c.1980.* Left to right: *Tina Cornish, Darby Ash, Frank Penny, Mark Govier, Colin Jones;* on the pole: *Neil Penny.*

Left: *Four young winners with their trophies at Stogumber Show, held in the newly-refurbished Village Hall, 2002. Left to right, back row: Sam Worrall (aged 6) and Kate Taylor (13); front: Emily Worrall (8) and Milly Taylor (11).*

Below: *Adults' pancake race at Sawpits Close, Stogumber, c.1980s.* Left to right: *Carolyn Kirk, David Kirk, Brenda Pitt, Kathleen Sellick, Peter Wilson, Kathryn Wilson, Pauline Sellick. The children are Lucy Pitt (with dog), Jonathan Pitt, Helen Sellick, Gemma Wilson, Belinda Sellick, Ben Wilson.*

Above left: *Presentation of Bibles at the Stogumber Christmas Tree Party, 1966.* Left to right: *Revd Paul Ashwin, Trevor Hutchings, Sheila Criddle, Christopher Comer.*

Above: *Pancake Day races, 1999.* Children participating include: *Aster Purdey, Christine Mills, Kimberley Penny, Samantha Hole, Mark Harris, Elizabeth Fallon, Ruth Hancox, Chris Weetch;* teachers: *Christine Mills, Ingrid Galliver, Hilary Biffen.*

Right: *Palm Sunday procession up Brook Street, Stogumber, 1991.*

❧ *Extracts from Stogumber VC First School Log-books, 1864–1953* ❧
The following extracts were taken by Margo Bunting and Marie Scarborough in 1983. No names have been mentioned here where embarrassment might be caused, and only initials have been inserted in certain places. The log-books are kept at the Somerset Record Office at Taunton. Owing to the 50-year rule, we are unable to publish further extracts. In March 1968 the Chief Education Officer met managers and parents to discuss the possible closure of the school in view of the low number of pupils attending, but due to the efforts of parents, staff, etc., it did not close; long may it remain open.

Chief teacher: Mary Jane Smyth – 2nd Class, 2nd Year A. Monitors (Diocesan): Jane Lovell, Jemima Lovell, Martha Tuckfield. Water was fetched daily, towels and soap kept and dirty children made to wash.

1864

4 Jan. Mr Trevelyan took the reading lesson – Miss Trevelyan also helped.

20 Jan. 4th Class poor at arithmetic – timetable needs alteration.

1 Feb. Admitted a boy of 11 unable to say his alphabet.

3 Feb. 2nd Class kept in for disorder during reading lesson – Miss Smyth considered it the fault of the teacher.

21 March Boy accidentally broke his slate.

12 April One of the boys whom I had occasion to punish attempted to take the cane from my hand. I was obliged to push him into the coalhouse where I kept him the whole of the dinner-time.

20 April Only 40 children in attendance – others ill with the measles.

9 May Most children recovered excepting their voices, being only able to speak in a whisper yet.

30 May Only 24 children owing to its being Club Day.

24 June We discovered that one of the boys had told a falsehood.

16 Nov. One of the 2nd Class girls left to attend another school in the parish as her uncle does not consider a National School respectable.

1865

15 Feb. I found two boys playing marbles in the playground instead of being in the schoolroom.

7 March One of the parents sent me word that her child was not to take home lessons.

28 April Attendance very small the whole day – children engaged in the fields.

8 May Attendance very small this morning owing to a fair in the parish. Summer holiday – then called 'Harvest Holiday'.

21 Sept. Attendance very small – only 50 children present owing to the weather.

1866

26 Feb. Several children punished for not walking orderly through the churchyard.

23 March Attendance very good – average this week 115–116.

11 May Attendance poor, 83.

18 June Only 46 children – many of them being employed in the fields.

20 Sept. Severely punished a boy for swearing. Several children punished for dirty faces – some sent home to brush their hair and make themselves tidy.

1867

Jan. Quite impossible to begin regular work – some children no boots, others ill, most afraid of the weather.

12 June One parent complained of the number of lessons her child had to learn at home.

21 June 80 children present – attendance very poor really.

12 July Arithmetic poor throughout the school.

22 Oct. Soap missed and then found in the pocket of a boy.

8-18 Nov. Several boys asked leave to work in the fields.

1868

22 Jan. Dinner stolen and eaten by little boy.

27 Feb. Knitting commenced in 1st Class.

9 Oct. Miss Smyth left school today. Jane Lovell commenced work alone.

1869

Jan. New mistress – Miss Lovell gone to Williton.

4 Jan. Punished S.H. for laughing during prayers. 84 in morning, 87 in afternoon.

23 Feb. Attendance scanty owing to a snowstorm.

1870

4 July Admitted George Tuckfield.

13 June Many children absent picking whortleberries.

1871

4 March Admitted Ellen Williams and Mary Anne Tuckfield.

1 May Obliged to assemble in a barn – schoolroom being enlarged. Lessons very inconvenient and very cold.

4 May Eliza Lovell obliged to teach a class at home – the barn not large enough.

10 May Children inattentive – watching birds building nests in the roof and rats.

14 July No 1st Class children present – all picking whortleberries.

25 Sept. Admitted James and Elizabeth Criddle.

9 Oct. Attendance not good – parents taking up their potatoes.

1872

6 May Stogumber Fair.

11 Dec. Squire Notley buried today.

1873

13 Jan. Elizabeth Bryant admitted.

4 Nov. Most of the children away picking apples.

1874

Jan. John Rowe, a certificated teacher, took charge of the Stogumber National School.

27 May Eliza Lovell (pupil-teacher, 4th year) left to take charge of a school of her own.

3 Aug. Many children away on account of gleaning.

21 Oct. Several absent – gone gathering acorns.

1875

19 March Very full school – between 120 and 130 all week.

15 April Some away potato planting.

12 Nov. Apple picking has again caused absence this week.

1876

24 Jan. 102 present. Report of H.M. Inspector: '... the children talk and copy from one another too much. The three elder standards are good.'

23 May Monksilver Club – several absent.

10 Aug. Children in the fields picking corn.

5 Dec. On the advice of Dr Crocker, the school is closing owing to the fever.

1877

2 March No school this afternoon – Confirmation at the Church.

18 June Mrs Jones assisted in sewing class.

1878

20 June Dismissed the children – told not to attend until further notice.

1 July Stogumber National School reopened by Henry C. Gladstone.

5 Oct. All children at school on time marked with red ink, late ones in black ink.

14 Nov. Reading unsatisfactory owing to supply of books being insufficient.

10 Dec. Attendance not good – many children have chilblains.

1879

13 Jan. Mr Sully put up some hat pegs and there are now pegs for 80 to 110 children.

3 March Two boys came to school without fees, for which they were sent home. They were absent all week. Staff consists of two pupil-teachers and one master – insufficient.

29 March Whooping cough is prevalent in the village.

12 May Average attendance 136.2 for the week.

2 June 162 children on the books.

1880

2 Feb. New rule – no child admitted after

9.10, so good attendance this week.

2 June   Gertrude Mary Hill commenced as monitress.

11 Nov.   George Timlett stood too close to classroom fire – leg rather severely burned. An accident.

1881

11 Aug.   Taunton Flower Show – only 42 in morning.

1882

27 July   Temperance fête in village.

5 Aug.   Four children have 'ringworm'.

9 Oct.   John Wedlake commenced duties as monitor at 1s. per week.

1883

16 April   Miss L. Symons commenced duties as infant and sewing mistress.

8 Aug.   Children away owing to Minehead Races.

1884

20 Nov.   J.W. stumbled and sat down on fire – set his trousers on fire and burned his leg. A guard necessary.

1885

24 April   Smallpox in Kingswood (15 children). Four with whooping cough.

15 May   Kingswood children back at school.

11 June   School fees must be increased.

14 Sept.   Average attendance 148 children.

25 Sept.   Flogged J.J. for playing truant.

1886

13 Jan.   Assembled school in afternoon half an hour later than usual owing to the funeral for a respected inhabitant of the village (Mr J.L. Cornish).

20 Jan.   A snow storm after the children got in school – sent for bread.

21 Dec.   St. Thomas's Day – Begging Day with the poorer folk in the village. As there were so many children absent begging, there was a holiday in the afternoon.

1887

19 Jan.   S.S. fell in the yard and ran one knitting needle through her leg and two others part ways... We sent for a doctor.

16 March The snow being about a foot deep, did not open school today.

21 June   Holiday – Queen's Jubilee celebrated by a feast in the schoolroom.

1 July   Whooping cough is very prevalent – each day some children are taken ill at school.

1888

28 March A good many children absent this week with bad colds and bad feet.

11 April   Told children whom I noticed had the ringworm badly to stay at home.

11 June   Report of HM Inspector: 'Decidedly good school... infants need desks... H.J. Mouncher, chief teacher; H.J. Wedlake, ex-PT; Dora Matthews, PT of year; Lucy Symons, assistant mistress.

14 June   Thrashed B.P. for wilfully throwing a stone at another boy in my presence

Stogumber School, 1896. Standing on the left is Mr Hollis (headmaster).

while in the playground.

August   Infants' desks now provided.

1889

8 March   An awfully wet day. Stopped work at 12.15 and waited for an opportunity to send the children home. The last batch left at 3.30 in the face of terrible rain. I found afterwards that some did not reach home till 8p.m. on account of the floods.

18–23 March   Harold Hyett (monitor) absent sick.

April   Mumps prevalent. Many children away with mumps, others from fear of them.

16 July   Minehead Races and whortleberry picking left us a poor attendance.

Nov.   Children suffering from a breaking-out about the head.

1890

6 Jan.   School opened this morning... poor attendance due to it being a very wet morning and old Christmas Day.

13 Jan.   Note from a parent at Vellow saying that children of a neighbour had some disease which she believed to be the 'itch'.

7 May   Sent in my resignation to the Managers.

24 June   Richard Rook is to assist as monitor, his school fee remitted.

27 June   My engagement terminates. New chief teacher: Walter N. Greg.

4 July   The paupers are paid for at a farthing per attendance, the rest a penny per week. Amounts: Paupers 7s.2d., non-paupers 2s.11d.

8 Aug.   On Monday M.W. wrote indecent words in a neighbour's book and told several lies to hide his fault. On Tuesday he was detained in the dinner hour by way of punishment but escaped through a window. On Thursday he was severely caned and again detained whilst the rest of the boys were

lectured in the playtime on the wickedness and filthiness of such language.

26 Sept.   Yesterday F.P. had to be severely punished for being purposely 25 minutes late in the afternoon.

1891

27 May   A.B. has had to be punished for lying – two strokes on the right hand, one on the left hand and two in another place.

28 May   R. Rook, monitor, leaves today. His place will be taken by H. Bidgood.

23 Oct.   W. and E. Hyett go to Taunton to compete for a County Scholarship under the Technical Instruction Scheme.

27 Nov.   Half day holiday as numbers had not fallen below 120 through the week.

1892

15 Jan.   Attendance poor – ground sheeted with ice.

5 Feb.   The room has been cold, not been able to have more than one fire on account of the smoke.

22 July   Attendance only 79 out of 120. Student teacher has measles.

12 Sept.   Medical Office of Health ordered closure of school for five weeks owing to a measles epidemic.

14 Oct.   Total attendance 28; reason – pouring rain.

1883

27 Jan.   Some fresh cases of ringworm and broken chilblains.

18 April   Holiday in afternoon – many children having gone to circus at Williton.

22 Sept.   W. Hyett entered Huish School at Taunton as a County Council scholar.

1884

8 Jan.   George Arthur Hollis began duty as master of this school.

27 July   More than 60% absent on account of the whort harvest principally – school closed.

Stogumber School in Edwardian times.

28 Sept. Miss L. Symons, cert. assistant infant mistress, left today. School funds will not allow the retention of her services.

1885

14 Sept. Miss G. Hill took charge of infants for the first time.

1896

2 April The drawing report received today – Excellent has been awarded for the third time in succession.

1897 *Government report: 'This is a decidedly well-taught school, etc.'*

24 May A poor school owing to the Agricultural Show at Minehead.

26 June School closed Tuesday and Wednesday on account of the celebrations of the Queen's Diamond Jubilee.

1898

28 Feb. A great deal of snow fell – only 8 children by 9 o'clock – school closed for day.

5 Aug. G.A. Hollis resigns as head teacher.

12 Sept. George Harold Gendall new head teacher.

14 Oct. Average attendance 90.

1899

6 March Many infants away owing to whooping cough.

25 April Owing to a concert in aid of Cricket Club funds, children dismissed at 1p.m. for the day.

27 Oct. Children encouraged to ask questions on the war in South Africa.

14 Nov. The School Attendance Committee now say that no child shall leave school until the age of 14 is attained, unless exempted.

17 Nov. Fires started this week.

1900

9 May G.H. Gendall gives three months' notice of resignation.

24 May Half holiday this afternoon in honour of Mafeking being relieved.

27 June Certain lads are absent pea-picking.

10 Sept. George P. Fevre commenced duties as master.

26 Sept. A first standard boy was found taking the elastic out of the girls' hats.

15 Oct. School closed for a month for an outbreak of measles.

1901

22 Jan. Her Most Gracious Majesty Queen Victoria died at Osborne.

1902

2 June Half holiday on the occasion of peace being proclaimed in South Africa.

30 June Commenced school after one week's vacation owing to Coronation festivities.

1903

16 Sept. Stogumber Sports Day.

21 Dec. This is 'Begging Day', but I am glad to say very few children have gone.

1904

Jan. W.J. Bidgood appointed assistant at £35 per year.

3 March W.J. Bidgood has left.

5 July Drill suspended as weather is very hot.

1905

7 July Attendance still very small owing to chickenpox.

6 Nov. A fire broke out in the village at a house occupied by Mr H. Hill, the bigger boys are carrying water for the engine.

1906

13 Jan. The full title of the school will be 'Somerset County Council: Stogumber Church of England School No. 379.'

11 June Only Miss Holcombe, monitor, and myself here.

2 July Miss Rawlins commences duties in school.

10 Sept. Children blackberry picking.

1907

28 Jan. A waterpipe has burst on east wall of school . . . several children in the infants' room were crying with the cold.

6 June Four boys punished for trespassing after gooseberries.

28 June Miss Rawlins leaves.

16 Oct. The new Vicar called – the Reverend E.A. Couch, B.A.

1908

16 April Harold White, aged 10 years, died today.

1909

28 April Circus in village.

24 May Empire Day – the National Anthem was sung.

25 July Church Sunday School treat at Blue Anchor.

1910

10 Feb. Three boys punished for lighting a fire in Old Way – a rick was burned down.

6 May H.M. King Edward VII died at Buckingham Palace.

12 July Great excitement this morning – a balloon passed over Stogumber.

1911

16 June School closed for one week for Coronation holiday.

1912

29 Jan. Very cold in school – temperature at 11a.m. 44 degrees.

1913

4 Sept. 104 this morning.

1914

1 Sept. Several boys away harvesting as labour is short owing to the war.

1915

23 Sept. Cookery lessons commenced.

4 Nov. Private Wescombe, an old pupil, called at the school on a short leave from the front.

10 Nov. No fire in school – bitterly cold.

1916

14 July School closed till 24 July for whortleberry picking.

1917

23 Oct. School closed for one and a half days for jumble sale.

1918

3 Oct. Half holiday for blackberry picking.

11 Nov. Armistice signed with Germany.

1919

5 May New infant teacher appointed.

1920 During the holidays the walls have been cleaned.

1921

13 Sept. The interior of the school has been re-decorated and a new stove provided in the main room.

1922

28 Feb. Holiday for the wedding of Princess Mary.

1923

26 April School closed for the wedding of H.R.H. Prince George.

1924

21 Jan. Railway strike – boys unable to go to Watchet for manual class.

1925

28 July One girl excluded – dirty head.

1926

13 Aug. School closed for alterations to premises.

1927

14 Feb. School closed for influenza.

1928

21 June W.I. outing to Torquay – several children absent in consequence.

1929

11 Sept. Manual class commenced at Williton.

1930

16 July One girl awarded a free place at Minehead County School.

1931

21 Jan. Stogumber Historic Pageant – school closed half day.

8 July Poor attendance – W.I. outing to Blue Anchor.

1932

10 Oct. Dairy class being held this week.

1933

13 Sept. School closed for centenary celebrations.

1934

29 Nov. School closed on occasion of the marriage of H.R.H. Duke of Kent and Princess Marina of Greece.

1935

6 May School closed for Silver Jubilee celebrations.

17 June J.M. Sidewell took temporary charge of school.

1936 The vexed question of the fires has been solved.

28 Jan. School closed. Funeral of H.M. King George V.

3 Feb. Mrs Georgina Russell started work as head teacher. Average attendance 56.

2 Oct. Permission granted to start milk scheme.

16 Oct. 51 children now having milk.

1937

14 May School closed for Coronation.

1938

22 Dec. School closed by order of the managers – all water services frozen.

1939

7 Jan. Still problems with the fires that smoke and very cold rooms.

24 Jan. The Vicar kindly sent in two big oil stoves.

1 Sept. Children assembled and gas masks were fitted.

3 Sept. War declared.

11 Sept. 13 evacuees admitted.

1940

19 Jan.–4 Feb. School closed, no water, six inches of snow, ice-bound roads.

5 Feb. School re-opened, water supply normal.

20 May Children drilled in running to shelter should a raid occur. All gas masks examined.

20 June Evacuees started school in the Church Hall.

27 Sept. Air raid warning at 11.35 when all children took shelter. All clear rung at 12.15.

2 Dec. Severe epidemic of measles. No fires, adverse wind.

1941

5 May Evacuee schoolchildren sent to this school. There is not sufficient seating accommodation, now 101 on books.

15 Oct. Senior girls gone out to gather hips.

1942

13 Jan. There is no blackout material, so fires cannot be lit early.

26 Jan. Blackout curtain put up at weekend.

School centenary celebrations, 1933. Mr George P. Fevre (head) is on the far left and the Revd E. Ambrose Couch (vicar) on the far right. Among the pupils are Ron Hayes, Harold Bryant, Cecil Bryant, Hector Potter, Joan Williams, John Hutchings, Joyce and June Parsons, Marion Lewis, Alfie Chidgey, Ted Routley, Ken Stockwell, Maurice Bryant, Douglas Clark, Kathleen Somerfield, Daniel Bailey, Harry Lewis, Joyce Bailey, Margaret Routley, Iris Taylor, June Hutchings, Ethel Eslick, W. Taylor, Mervyn Stockham, Chris Sansom, Jack Bryant.

Right: *Stogumber School senior girls, 1944. Among those pictured are: Miss Strangwood (teacher), Joan Bryant, Audrey Jones, Barbara Tremlett, Ivy Fox, Joan Davey, Rosa May, Lucy Bellringer, Pam Hole, Sylvia Watts.*

Below: *Three Stogumber teachers, 1944. Left to right: Miss Rosemary Allen, Mrs Doreen Morse, Miss Joan Strangwood.*

Stogumber School, late 1940s.

25 Feb. Children came for milk and then went home. Pipes burst – even Church Hall below freezing.

7 Aug. Mrs Russell retires, aged 65.

7 Sept. Joan Strangwood appointed headmistress.

24 Sept. H.M. Inspector's visit. He welcomed use of wireless to supplement studies and for musical appreciation.

10 Nov. The pipe of the stove nearest the door became red hot, caught the blackout curtain which became aflame. A boy tore it down and stamped upon it... little damage in consequence, but the loss of the curtain.

1943

19 Jan. House system started: Reds, Quantock; Greens, Brendons.

10 May Opening day of our School Wings for Victory Week – £268 raised.

19 May Gramophone purchased for school use.

18 Oct. 35 children took hot dinners at school.

1944

6 March 62 children. Head teacher took both juniors and seniors together.

30 March School closed for induction of new Vicar, the Reverend W.J.P. Cox.

8 May First day of Salute the Soldier Campaign.

12 May We raised £110.1s. for Salute the Soldier.

6 June D-Day landings on Normandy beaches by Allied Forces.

8/9 Dec. Nativity Play – £17 for wireless.

1945

23 Jan. Heavy snow – no hot dinners came, dismissed school early.

26 Jan. Attendance drops to 18.

10 April School opened after Easter holidays – 51 Somerset children, 18 evacuees.

7 May In the evening scholars old and new gathered together to ring the school bell in honour of victory in Europe. Mr Fevre began the ringing.

8/9 May School closed in honour of victory.

5 Oct. Joan Strangwood (head teacher) relinquished her post owing to her forthcoming marriage to a missionary.

30 Oct. School closed for half term plus VJ Day.

12 Nov.   Vera Baxter appointed head teacher.

1946

8 Jan.   Seniors now removed to Williton School.

1947

29 Jan.   Heavy fall of snow – only 6 present.

31 Jan.   Miss Baxter resigned as head teacher owing to appointment as head teacher at Rugby.

3 Feb.   Vera Watson takes temporary charge of school.

20 Feb.   Weather shows no sign of improving – water frozen in lavatory pans and all milk in bottles frozen.

25 Feb.   The last two nights have been the coldest for a decade.

3 March   Mr Jackman took charge.

6 and 7 March   School closed – unapproachable for snowdrifts.

13 June   Mr Jackman's duties terminated.

16 June   Hilda Dale appointed head teacher.

8 Sept.   37 children on roll.

19 Nov.   School closes tomorrow on the occasion of the wedding of H.R.H. Princess Elizabeth.

1948

9 March   This dinnertime a dog came into the playground and bit a girl's leg.

23 July   Many children have stayed away to go to the circus at Taunton.

1949

14 July   Sudden heavy rains have caused floods – 18 children absent in consequence.

1950

15 Dec.   Snow drifts – no children from Vexford.

1951

May   Festival of Britain.

24 May   12 children were taken to Windsor Castle.

1952

6 Feb.   H.M. King George VI died.

19 Dec.   Hilda Dale (head teacher) relinquishes her post.

1953

5 Jan.   Grace Albiston, supply teacher, takes charge – 29 out of 35 being present.

20 April   Mary F. Chipp commenced duties as head teacher.

1, 2, 3 June   Special holiday for Coronation of H.M. Queen Elizabeth II.

Left: *School centenary celebrations, 1933. Left to right: ?, Ethel Eslick, Betty Hayes, Iris Taylor, Barbara Criddle, June Hutchings, Margaret Routley, Joyce Parsons, Enid Trebble, June Parsons, Marion Lewis, Vera Taylor.*

Stogumber CE School, 1936. Left to right, back row: Mrs Calloway, P. Tuckfield, T. Besley, W. Gadd, D. Maddock, Chris Sansom, R. Hayes, J. Bryant, M. Stockham, D. Clark, C. Stevens, E. Eslick, Miss Ricardo; fourth: Vera Taylor, Iris Gulliford, E. Bellringer, ?, M. Lewis, R. Bucknell, C. Trebble, H. Potter, A. Chidgey; third: Tim Bellringer, J. Parsons, L. Gulliford, D. Bailey, D. Walford, G. Criddle, R. Hutchings, H. Lewis, K. Lewis, T. Routley, J. Parsons, J. Hutchings, B. Stevens, L. Eames; second, sitting: M. Bryant, P. Ebbage, J. Westcott, M. Routley, J. Bryant, B. Criddle, P. Maddock, Mrs M.A. Russell (headmistress), I. Taylor, E. Trebble, ? Gulliford, G. Ebbage, D. Davey, K. Clark; front: K. Stockwell, J. Hayes, F. Maddock, E. Walford, T. Routley, Mary Sansom, J. Ebbage, D. Maddock, Colin Sansom, R. Bucknell.

Left: *Stogumber School, 1968. Left to right, back row: Mrs Howe (head teacher), Francis Penny, Andrew Hayes, Clive Davey, Stephen Holcombe, Kevin Hill, ?; third: Susan Hutchings, Kathy Cook, Wendy Penny, Pam Book, Pamela Thompson; second: P. Lobb, Robin Illingworth, Duncan Trigg, Simon Pearce, ?; front: James Illingworth, John Hawkins, ?, Dean Waller, Derek Howe, Neil Penny.*

Right: *Stogumber School, c.1970. Left to right, back row: ?, Mrs Toal, Adrian Hoyle, H. Campbell, Susan Hutchings, S. Holcombe, S. Campbell, Wendy Bryant, Frank Penny, Nigel Richards, Miss Storr, Marjorie Maddock; third: ?, B. Tabrett, S. Hoyle, S. Campbell, A. Thompson, Derek Howe, ?, Paul Webb, Wendy Richards, Julia Sims; second: Rob Hayes, K. Hoyle, Dean Waller, Kevin Hares, Tracey Howe,*

Alison Toal, Janice Hayes, Elaine Webb; front: ?, ?, David ('Noddy') Bryant, Paul Bryant, ?, Andy Bryant.

Below: **Nativity play, 1984. Included are: Gregory Scott, Jonathan Pitt, Richard Berry, Nicola Williams, Donna Ryder, two girls named Scarborough, Stephanie Ryder, Natalie Williams, Denise Brown, Geoffrey Cross, ? Pitt, Wayne Sawyer, ? De Wolf.**

Above: *Pupils at Stogumber First School gained an insight into the French way of life and learned a little of the language from French student Quentin Molet, who was on a cultural exchange at the school during the autumn term of 2002. Left to right, back row: Anita Appleby, Janet Harbour, Claire Wheeler, Becky Hooper, Quentin Molet; front: pupils Oliver Greenslade, Tom Lile, Lucy Hill, Cameron Sandford, Julian Harding, Charlie Melvin-Sparks.*

Above: *Stogumber School and Playgroup, 2001.* **Left to right, back row:** *Shirley Sully, Elizabeth Storrs-Fox, Alice Penny, Mark Hayes, Rebecca Franklin, Edward Thomas, Margaret Storrs-Fox;* **fourth:** *Peta-Ann Livermoore, Anita Appleby, Georgia Denot, Zack Ryder, Ailish Hoggart, Clare Tarr, Eli Hayes, Aidan Johnson, Mark Bryant, Ryan Reacord, Olivia Coles, Jan Harbour, Shane Booker, Annie Swannack, Celia Bebb;* **third:** *Andrew Scott, Francesca Walker, Matthew Sharpe, Jessica Ware, Elizabeth Fallon, Ruth Hancock, Jade Hill, Tom Lile, Tristan Reacord, Danny Wilson;* **second:** *Joy Bell, Alistair and Cameron Weldon, Lucy Hill, Callum Tarr, River Speers, Chloe Pearson, ?, Cane Scott, Hannah Coles, Thomas Pearson, Evan Storrs-Fox, Brendon Timewell, Carole Giles;* **front:** *Tracey Thomas, Curtis Hole, Ryan Duncton, Victoria Coles, Lewis Scrimgeour, Chloe Scrimgeour, Chloe Kilworth, Amber Phillips, Matthew Pearson, Simon Scott.*

Background image: *Farewell gathering for Mrs Toal (holding bouquet), head os Stogumber First School, 1985.*

Right: *First School, 2000.* **Left to right, back row:** *Mrs Swannack, Joanne Hole, Becky Franklin, Brett Tarr, Mark Harris, Paul Timewell, Sarah-Jane Harris, Elizabeth Storrs-Fox, Damien Harris, Lee Penny, Elizabeth Fallon, Sarah Morrison, Mrs Storrs-Fox;* **middle:** *Clare Tarr, Andrew Harris, Eli Hayes, Tristan Reacord, Danny Wilson, Ruth Hancock, Alice Penny, Matthew Sharp, Vicky Oldfield, Jessica Ware, Francesca Walker, Tammy-Jade Hill, Gabriel Purdey;* **front:** *Ailish Hoggart, Eva Van-Aalen, Ryan Reacord, Alastair Weldon, Kane Scott, Mrs Giles, Chloe Pearson, Aidan Johnson, Mark Bryant, Georgia Denot, Shane Booker.*

Stogumber School swimming competition group, 1974. Left to right, back row: *Richard Heaton, Roger Webb, Robert Matthews, Claire Dyer, Beryl Pearson;* middle: *Joanne Waller, Julia Hill, Daniel Winkleigh, Louise Hoyle, Alison Toal, Maxine Waller;* front: *Robert Dyer, Graham Hill, ?, Martin Campbell, Martin Pearson.*

Stogumber CEVC First School, 1998. Left to right, back row: *Mrs Biffen, Mrs Mills, Florence England, Christopher Weetch, Kirstin Barnes, Samantha Hole, Timothy Cavey, Victoria Butler, Edward Storrs-Fox, Kimberley Penny, Joshua Waygood, Mrs Swannack;* middle: *Elizabeth Storrs-Fox, Elizabeth Fallon, Lee Penny, Joanne Hole, James Pearson, Ruth Hancock, Alice Penny, Aster Purdey, Alison Watts, Sarah-Jane Harris;* front: *Gabriel Purdey, Mark Harris, Vicky Oldfield, Francesca Walker, Mrs Ingrid Galliver, Lawrence Griffiths, Andrew Scott, Rebecca Franklin, Robert Turner.*

Top: *View of Stogumber from Ashbeer, late 1940s.*

Above left: *High Street, showing the old Post Office, c.1960.*

Above right: *Cottage in Hill Street, Stogumber, c.1950s.*

Below: *Stogumber from Togford Hill, c.1920.*

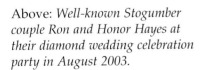

Above: *Well-known Stogumber couple Ron and Honor Hayes at their diamond wedding celebration party in August 2003.*

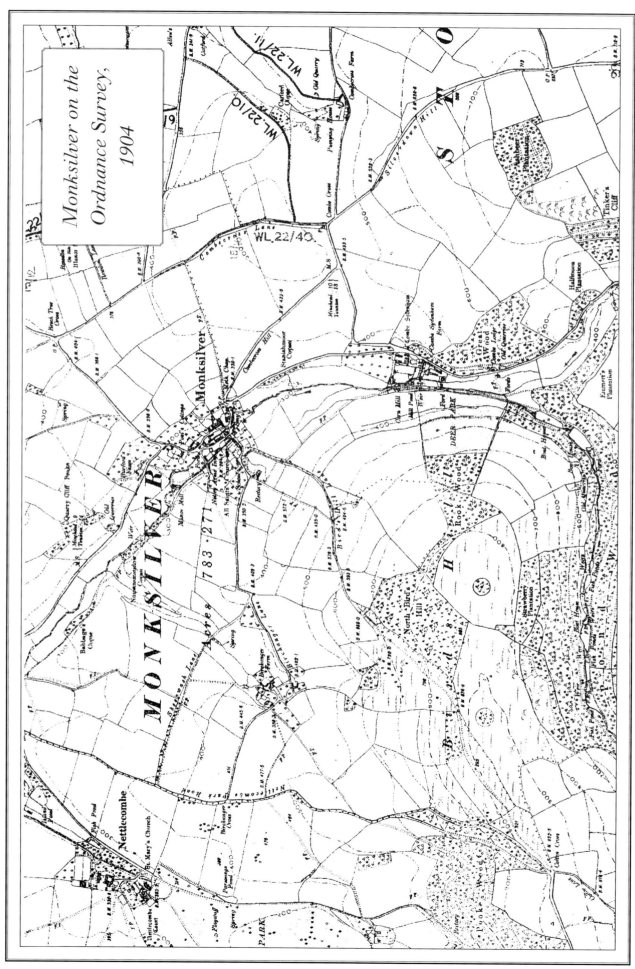

Monksilver on the
Ordnance Survey,
1904

Two

Monksilver

The quaint and idyllic village of Monksilver with its colour-washed houses and cottages is situated one-and-a-half miles west of Stogumber, within the eastern perimeter of Exmoor National Park. The scenic valley road through the parish was turnpiked in 1765 as part of the route from Taunton to Minehead, and the road through Monksilver village was adopted in 1806 as part of the Wiveliscombe turnpike road to Watchet.

Until the fourteenth century the parish was called Silver, from the Latin 'silva', indicating a wooded district. Silver was also the original name of the stream which falls into the sea at Doniford. After this the parish was called Silver Monachorum or Monksilver after its association with Goldcliff Priory and the monks in Monmouthshire. In 1831 the village population stood at 322, but then declined rapidly; it numbered 130 in 1981 and 100 in 2001.

West Somerset Foxhounds at Monksilver.

The Parish Church of All Saints is a little gem, some parts dating from the twelfth century. The tower is fourteenth century and there were additions and alterations made in the late-fifteenth century when the nave was rebuilt and the south aisle and chapel were added. Legend has it that the south aisle was built from funds provided by a blacksmith who had chanced upon a sack full of gold. The story goes that a local blacksmith sent to Bristol for a hundredweight of iron. In due course he received a sack filled with metal and upon opening it was astonished to find it full of gold. A window in the south aisle includes stained glass depicting blacksmith's tools – hammer, nail, a pair of pincers and a horseshoe. However, this story has been somewhat disputed since it was discovered that claw hammers were unknown before the 1800s and that the stained glass was in fact the work of John Toms, of Wellington, an expert of the craft during the mid-nineteenth century.

During his incumbency from 1915–27 the Revd R.H. Gardner-McTaggart was responsible for much good work in the parish, and as a tribute to him a Madonna was placed in the church by his family. In more recent times a desk was given in memory of a loyal servant of the church, Herbert Edwin Davis, and Eva Jane Davis.

Many of the ancient pews have carved bench ends depicting a stag, sheep, fish, flowers, sprays of leaves and a candlestick. The list of rectors dates from 1324 and the registers from 1653. There are five bells of varying ages; the second bell dates from about 1543 and the treble was given by George Notley. The bells were rehung in 1910 by John Sully, of Stogumber. The gargoyles on the south side are very old, one of which is supposed to represent someone suffering from toothache visiting a medieval dentist!

In the churchyard stands a large yew tree, said to have been planted by the village blacksmith in 1770, and among the graves are those of the Notley family, previous owners of Combe Sydenham. Outside the church door stands the famous headstone of the murdered Conibeers, the story of whom is referred to elsewhere in this book.

For over 300 years Combe Sydenham had been one of the homes of the Sydenham family. In 1796 the manor was bought by the Revd George Notley, then passed down to his descendants until being sold in the 1950s, when that family's 150 years of association with the estate came to an end. Members of the Notley family do, however, live in and around the village at the time of writing.

The Rectory was worth £9.15s.4d. in 1535 and £80 in 1668! In 1838 a new classic-style Rectory was built

Above: *Looking up High Street, Monksilver, in Victorian times.*

Left and below: *Laurel and Tudor Cottages, Monksilver, c.1950s, and, following restoration, in the 1960s.*

Above: *George Moore standing beside a felled tree trunk
at Monksilver, c.1950.*

Right: *Sweeping hay at
Beech Tree Cross, c.1937.*

Below: *View from the Rap.*

An Edwardian social gathering at Monksilver.

A woodland gathering in Edwardian times.

which was later sold, and in 1968 a new house was erected, now a private residence. Monksilver is now part of the seven-parish Quantock Towers Benefice.

In the 1890s Wesleyan Methodists were active in the parish, and a chapel constructed of corrugated iron was built in 1897, but has since closed. It still stands on the edge of the village just over the border in Stogumber parish.

The Manor Court Leet had jurisdiction in Monksilver and appears to have been held annually by the mid-fifteenth century; it was still in existence in the nineteenth century. It was served by a bailiff, a constable, a tithingman and a pound-keeper as its officers. Tithingmen served in rotation from the sixteenth century, with two churchwardens and two sidesmen also serving in the same way. By 1796 a poorhouse had been built and in 1836 Monksilver joined the Williton Poor Law Union. From 1894 the parish was part of Williton Rural District and from 1974 of West Somerset District; it has its own Parish Council.

Ale was sold in the parish in 1551 and in 1665 a tippling house was recorded. By 1675 there was a Ram Inn situated on the opposite side of the road to the Notley Arms, but this had been renamed the Half Moon by 1785. It subsequently became a private residence, lived in during the 1950s by an actor named William Devlin, who gave it the name by which it is still known today, Half Moon Cottage. In 1743 a Red Lion Inn was mentioned, which was later licensed as a Quaker meeting house. Finally, the Notley Arms was opened between 1861–66; an outstanding village feature is the Notley Arms coaching barn (later also known as the club room), which bears the date 1860.

There was a mill at Monksilver as far back as 1086, and milling still operated into the 1930s. The nineteenth-century mill and house survive, but its working parts have been removed. In the late-seventeenth and early-eighteenth centuries there were clockmakers in Monksilver, and the 1851 census listed drapers, grocers, harness-makers and straw bonnet-makers also at work here.

Local children attended a school at Nettlecombe in 1818, but day- and Sunday schools were started in Monksilver in 1825 with 45 children. A second day-school was opened in 1832 with 31 pupils on the roll. A new school, united with the National Society, was built in 1847 and took 58 boys and 31 girls. It was enlarged in 1870, being supported by a parish rate. The number of pupils totalled 30 in 1937, helped by an influx of children from Elworthy School upon the latter's closure. At the end of the Second World War pupils numbered 28, which included the children transferred from the Nettlecombe/Yarde School which closed in 1945. However, numbers began to dwindle and the school was closed in 1959, the children then being transferred to Williton. The school buildings became a private house.

It is worth including the following relating to Monksilver during the Second World War which comes from Jack Hurley's book, *Exmoor in Wartime*:

As for the observance of secrecy, we should salute, albeit with a smile, the common sense shown by the invasion committee for the grouped villages of Monksilver, Nettlecombe and Elworthy. They had to reply to a questionnaire sent out by the military. On a document marked 'Strictly Confidential' appeared the question, 'Where are your defence positions?' The minute book records this answer: 'We have stated our defence positions verbally to the military, but we have not written them down'!

Tools and plant available for an emergency are listed. Monksilver could produce 20 shovels and spades, 10 pickaxes and 10 wheelbarrows. These would be stacked at the Rectory until the 'action stations' signal was given. At Criddles Farm, Monksilver, Charlie Howe was supervising officer for emergency transport; he could call upon nine one-horse carts, three two-horse wagons and two tractors each with wagon. From outlying farms he could draw 18 horses, six tractors, 14 wagons and 16 carts. Field ovens for cooking communal meals would be set up in sunken lanes.

Obviously Monksilver has changed over the years with properties being modernised and well maintained, but it has retained the rustic charm shown in the old photographs. Perhaps the most significant changes have been the decrease in the number of people employed in agriculture and the increase of traffic through the village. The blacksmith's forge and nearby wheelwright/carpenter's workshop at the end of Front Street on the way to Combe Sydenham have long since ceased to function as such. The last blacksmith to work at the Monksilver forge was Herbert James Kerslake, a member of a well-known local family of farriers, who also operated forges at Washford and Williton, where he learnt his trade. Following Army service as a sergeant farrier during the First World War, Mr Kerslake took on the smithy at Monksilver, which he operated for 26 years until its closure in 1946. The last carpenters were Owen Allen & Son; Owen was a pillar of the Methodist Chapel and his son later became a minister.

Unfortunately, Monksilver lost its Post Office and general stores in the 1970s. Among former proprietors here were Edgar Farmer (who moved to Williton Post Office), Creedy, Jackson, Reed, Tipper and Bird. Another well-known Monksilver businessman was the late Ernest G. Bryant, who started a taxi service in the village in the 1930s, eventually moving to Williton and expanding to run a fleet of coaches and taxis which are still in existence. He was also a former landlord of the Notley Arms.

A great asset was added to the village in 1993 when the Elworthy, Monksilver and Nettlecombe Community Hall was opened after years of much fund-raising.

❧ *A Century of Village Views* ❧

Top: *Front Street, Monksilver, c.1905, showing Porch Cottage in the foreground, next to which was the former Half Moon Inn (later Half Moon Cottage); in the background is the Notley Arms.*

Above: *Looking down High Street, Monksilver, in Edwardian times.*

Above right: *Burfords (now Inglewood), Monksilver, c.1910.*

Right: *Edwardian mode of transport at Monksilver.*

Above: *Monksilver, c.1920s.*

Left: *Front Street, Monksilver, c.1930.*

Below: *Monksilver (note the leat), 1930s*

Right: *Monksilver, showing the old Methodist Chapel in the background.*

Below: *Cottages in Monksilver where Back Way joins the main road, 1946. Pictured are Anthony Blackmore and Shirley Webber.*

Bottom: *Monksilver, c.1948.*

Top left and right: *Monksilver Stream, late 1940s, before the bridge was built, and the stream covered by the bridge at Monksilver, 2002.*

Above: *Christmas-card scene at Monksilver in the 1990s.*

Above: *Chapel Corner, Monksilver, 1963.*

Right: *Half Moon Cottage (formerly the Half Moon Inn), Monksilver, 2002.*

Above: *Porch Cottage, Monksilver, 1972.*

Left: *Monksilver Methodist Chapel, mid-1980s (now closed).*

Below: *The shop and Post Office in the village, 1972.*

Above: *Hunt meet at the Notley Arms old coach-house, c.1930s.*

Right: *Pond Woods, Monksilver, c.1890.*

Below: *The village seen from the Notley Arms looking west, 1926.*

All Saints Church

All Saints Church, Monksilver.

Above: *The gargoyle at the church, reputed to depict a medieval dentist!*

Above right: *Blacksmith's tools depicted in stained glass in one of the south aisle windows of the Parish Church.*

Right: *One of the elaborate and ancient carved bench ends in the church.*

Far right: *Interior of All Saints.*

Above: *The rector and choirboys of Monksilver Parish Church, c.1930s.* Left to right, back: *Albert Snell, Fred Thorn, Cecil Potter, Revd Strother, George May, Peter Quartley;* front: *Donald Potter, Ray Davis.*

Right: *The Revd R.H. Gardner-McTaggart, Monksilver's rector, 1915–27.*

Monksilver Rectory, c.1905.

❧ *Village Trade* ❧

The Mill, Monksilver, c.1910.

Left: *Mr and Mrs Edgar Farmer, their daughter Marjorie and postman Bill Best outside Monksilver Post Office and shop in the 1920s. Mr Farmer was the sub-postmaster.*

Farrier Herbert Kerslake busy at his Monksilver forge, c.1940s. Holding the pony is Bill Date of Beggearn Huish.

Brian Somerfield outside Monksilver Post Office and shop, 1946.

Monksilver Glass Painting is based at the Old Schoolhouse in Monksilver and specialises in delightful artworks, produced using the eighteenth-century method of reverse glass painting. The company also runs training courses and supplies glass-painting kits by mail order for those who want to try their own hand at this historic technique. The company website can be found at www.reverseglasspainting.com

Above: *The welcoming and thriving Notley Arms, 2002, which has received many awards over the years, including runner-up in the Egon Ronay Pub of the Year competition and the* Good Pub Guide's *Landlord and Landlady of the Year for publicans Sarah and Alistair Cade.*

Left: *Reed being taken to the river at Monksilver for damping before being used for thatching, c.1941. Charlie Howe with horse and cart and thatcher W. Webber.*

Above main: *Tom Stark muck spreading with Malcolm Ash on the tractor at Birchanger Farm, Monksilver, c.1950s.*

Above inset: *Tom Stark driving a Titan 10/20 tractor powered by oil engine at Birchanger Farm, c.1940.*

Above: *Tom Stark with horses and mowing machine at Birchanger Farm, Monksilver, in the late 1940s.*

Left: *Birchanger Farm, Monksilver, 1909.*

Left: *Sheep dipping at Monksilver, c.1955. Left to right: George Tuckfield, Tom Stark, ?.*

Below: Left to right: *John Notley, Verna Notley, Horace Notley and Tom Stark at Birchanger Farm, Monksilver, c.1950s.*

Left: *Derek Watts at the wheel of a combine harvester at Birchanger, c.1960. With him are Tom and Emily Stark.*

Below: *Harvest time at Birchanger, 1949. Derek Watts is the lad on the cart.*

Criddles Farmhouse, 1904.

Right: *A lot of bull at Criddles Farm, Monksilver, in 1951! Left to right: Rex Howe, Charles Howe and Ken Stephens with three Devon bulls prior to being taken to Exeter bull sale.*

Below: *Enie Howe bottle-feeding a lamb and kitten at Monksilver, late 1940s.*

Back Way, Monksilver, with Criddles Farm on the left, c.1920.

Harvesting and reed-combing, 1965. Ruth Howe and Rover with her father Rex behind.

Above: *Early harvest at Monksilver, 12 July 1987. Andrew Howe on combine harvester, Adrian Hill driving tractor.*

Selecting lambs at Monksilver for market, c.1988. **Left to right: Christine, Andrew and Rex Howe.**

Charlie Howe with his prize-winning 'Red Ruby' Devon bull outside Criddles, 1932.

An aerial view of Monksilver, c.1990.

Left: *Montague Notley on Whiteface at the new Burfords (now Inglewood), c.1910. The horse later went to war and was one of the few to return.*

Background image: *Devon 'Red Ruby' cattle grazing at Burfords, c.1930s.*

Above: *Montague Notley (centre), holding Violet and Percy Notley, with farm workers at Burfords, c.1908.*

Background image: *Pea-picking at Monksilver, 1986.*

❧ Village Faces ❧

Left: *Henry Langdon outside his home in Mill Lane; he was born at Monksilver in 1835. Henry's father was Martin Langdon, who died at Birds Hill Lane in 1841. His mother was Sarah Flower Howe, who was born at Stogumber in 1797 and died in 1870.*

Below: *Arthur Thorn, of Monksilver, astride his OK Junior motorcycle in 1921.*

Below left: *Mr and Mrs H. Hooper going to record their votes at Monksilver at the 1979 General Election. A caravan was used as the polling station.*

Reg Ridler with carthorses Farmer, Duke and Flower at Monksilver, 1932.

❧ *Calloways* ❧

Above: *Herbert Hall and Frank Calloway* (both far right, sitting), *of Monksilver, before departing with other recruits for military service in the First World War. Sitting in the centre is Sergeant Bert Davis.*

Left: *Edgar Calloway, known as 'Roc', c.1969.*

Above: *Jane Calloway, wife of William, of Monksilver, c.1905.*

Right: *William Calloway, of Back Way, with his grandson Gordon Hall, c.1926.*

Above: *Bosleys Band from Tolland at Monksilver, 1906. Among those pictured are John Bosley, Sid Slocombe, ? Dyte, Harry Bosley, Albert Bosley, Bill Bosley, Lord St Audries, ? King.*

Right: *Celebrating VE Day at Monksilver in fancy dress, 1945. Left to right: Heather Potter, Len Stephens, Donald Potter.*

Gathering at Monksilver to celebrate the millennium.

Local Personalities

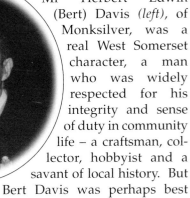

The late Herbert E. Davis: Mr Herbert Edwin (Bert) Davis *(left)*, of Monksilver, was a real West Somerset character, a man who was widely respected for his integrity and sense of duty in community life – a craftsman, collector, hobbyist and a savant of local history. But Bert Davis was perhaps best known of all as the old soldier, 'Terrier' and Volunteer, whose links with service to his country went back no less than 76 years. He took the Queen's Shilling in 1893 when he enlisted in the 9th Rifle Volunteers. Mr Davis had a natural aptitude for soldiering and went to great pains to master the subject by attending every possible course on military matters. This often entailed the long journey to Taunton on a bicycle and a stay there over the weekend in order to learn all he could at the barracks. Mr Davis later joined the Territorial Army with the 1/5th Battalion of the Somerset Light Infantry and, with the outbreak of war in 1914, went to India and the Middle East (by which time he was RSM of the Battalion) and ended his soldiering with commissioned rank.

The Davis military association is very remarkable, extending from his father's (Mr Edwin Davis, of Yarde) 30 years' service in the old Volunteers (from about the mid-1860s) to Bert's youngest son Ray, who attained the rank of lieutenant-colonel in the Royal Engineers; his other two sons also saw military service.

Spending his last 49 years at Monksilver, Mr Davis' sense of duty and responsibility made him an ideal parish man for many tasks on behalf of the community. But he had not entirely done with military matters. The Second World War found him in uniform again, this time as commander of Stogumber platoon of the Home Guard, and under his experienced leadership it became a highly efficient unit. Mr Davis was a founder-member of the Bicknoller branch of the Royal British Legion, doing his duties as secretary for many years, and from 1958 until 1965 he was its president.

In civilian life Mr Davis had been just as much a character, and his keen mind never deserted him. He was 72 when in 1949 Monksilver formed a Parish Council and chose him as its first chairman, and at the same time sent him to represent the parish on the old Williton Rural District Council, where he served for 13 years. He was a forthright champion of his village's interests, and the erection of a vehicular bridge over the river was a necessity for which he fought long and hard. He was a special constable for 11 years, and in all activities in Monksilver his interest was keen; he was also a churchwarden and school manager.

By trade a plumber and decorator, Mr Davis had skills which went much further, notably in restoration work on old properties. His private interests included military history, archaeology, local history and the collecting of antiques. At one time he possessed a remarkable collection of military medals. He was also a skilled wood carver, and many examples of his work still exist.

The eldest son of Mr and Mrs Edwin Davis, of Yarde, Bert Davis died in November 1969, aged 92.

The late Rex Howe: Donald Rex Howe *(below)* was born at Poole Town, Luxborough, his family moving to Criddles Farm, Monksilver, when he was seven years old. He was always keenly interested in farming, but unfortunately suffered ill-health for many of his later years, when the tricycle which he rode became something of a fixture in the local scenery. Before his father, Mr Charlie Howe (known to many as 'Uncle Char'), retired, their great interest was breeding 'Red Rubies' – North Devon cattle – and they were well known for their fine herd. They attained considerable success in this, sending one bull to Tasmania as well as exporting others for breeding purposes.

Later Rex developed a small milking herd and increased the arable and sheep production with the help of his family. He married Barbara Hosegood in 1952 and a year later took over the management of Criddles when his father retired.

Rex took a keen interest in country sports and had been a committee member and later an honorary vice-president of Dunster Show. He was also involved with the local Methodist Chapel, which has since closed.

Rex died in 1996, aged 74 years, and Criddles is farmed by his son Andrew.

Left: *The Elworthy, Monksilver and Nettlecombe Community Hall was opened in 1993 when Lady Elizabeth Gass, representing the people from the three parishes, received the keys to the hall on their behalf from Shaun Stacey, of Mike Stacey Builders. Don Creasey was chairman of the committee which spearheaded a six-year effort to raise funds for the £125,000 Community Hall sited at Monksilver. Some 130 villagers were present on the opening day to raise their glasses to success. It is widely used for a variety of social and sporting functions, including Monksilver Fête, also for business events and exhibitions, and is a great asset to the community.*

Left: *Lady Gass opening the Community Hall in 1993. On her left are Don Creasey and Shaun Stacey.*

Above: *Fancy dress at a Monksilver Fête, c.1955. Angela Young* (left) *and Peter Ridler.*

Right: *Fancy dress at the Fête, c.1957. Left to right: ?, Malcolm Blackmore, William Gulliford, Nancy Tuckfield, Barbara Symes, Em Stark, Marilyn Coles, Carol Stark.*

Below left and right: *Enjoying a Punch and Judy show and skittling for a pig at Monksilver Village Fête, 2002.*

❧ Country Fair ❧

Left: *Children enjoying the Monksilver Country Fair, 1993.*

Below, left: *Slow bicycle race.* Left to right: *Andrew Howe, John Foster, John Cotterill, Rex Howe.*

Below: *Greasy pole fight.* On the pole: *John Foster* (left) *and Andrew Howe;* spectators, left to right: *Paul Grellier, ?, Ruth Howe, Mrs Tarr, Christine Grellier.*

Left: *Pig roast at Monksilver Country Fair, 1993.* Left to right: *Bob Barron senr, Doris Barron, Gail Kidner, ?.*

Below: *Tug-of-war.* Left to right: *Andrew Howe, ?, Dan Cotterill, Danny Morgan, John Notley, Ernie Andrews, ?, Mr Turner, Mr Tarr, John Cotterill.*

✤ *Royal Occasions* ✤

Wilf Watts leading the Silver Jubilee parade at Monksilver in 1935.

Above: *Celebrating King George V's Silver Jubilee at Monksilver in 1935. Left to right: Ruby May, Fred Thorn, Nancy Bryant, Cecil Potter, George May.*

Right: *Fancy dress at Monksilver Coronation Day celebrations, 1953. Left to right: Mrs Gadd, Em Stark, Miss Piper, Geoff Ridler, Marjorie Ridler, Enie Howe.*

Celebrating King George V's Silver Jubilee at Monksilver in 1935.

Coronation Celebrations, 1953

Although a heavy downpour of rain meant that a sports programme had to be cancelled, children in the parish of Monksilver were amply provided for on Queen Elizabeth II's Coronation Day, Tuesday 2 June 1953. The celebrations commenced with a service at All Saints Church, conducted by the rector, the Revd R.P. Wickens, when each child received a memento in the form of a Bible, prayer book or card, given by a local gentleman. Before and after the service the church bells were rung by Messrs T. Upham (captain), E. Ash, J. Watts, J. Dymond, the Revd R.P. Wickens and Miss Heather Potter.

The cancelled sports had been due to be held in Little Hill, the arrangements being made by Messrs F.G. Ridler and F. Stevens, with Mr R. Howe (starter) and Mr Campbell-Voullaire (judge). Tea in the schoolroom for both adults and children was supervised by Mrs E.G. Bryant with the assistance of other ladies.

A highlight of the programme was a fancy-dress parade, judged by Miss Wickens, Miss Notley and Mr Bell. Winners were: Adults, 1st Mr and Mrs R. Howe, 2nd Miss E. Howe, 3rd Miss H. Potter and Mr F.G. Ridler (tie); children, 1st Jennifer Dymond, 2nd Carol Stark, 3rd Brian Stevens; best-decorated vehicle, 1st Derek Webb, 2nd Malcolm Ash, 3rd Peter and Angela Ridler. Mr Campbell-Voullaire (Combe Sydenham) made the presentation of souvenir mugs to the children and also the prizes for the fancy-dress parade.

The day's activities concluded with a social evening, Mrs A. Tuckfield conducting dancing and games to the accordion music of Mr J. Moore; Mr H. Hooper dispensed beer.

The arrangements for the celebrations were made by a committee comprising Mesdames E.G. Bryant, M.F. Chipp, A. Tuckfield, E. Stark, G. Potter, R. Howe, H. Hooper and Miss M. Davis, and Messrs H. Welch, G. Ridler, H.C.W. Howe, F.G. Stevens, P. Creedy, W. Shepherd, H. Hooper and H.E. Davis, as well as the Revd R.P. Wickens.

❧ *Plays & Parties* ❧

Above: *The Revd R.H. Gardner-McTaggart and cast members of the play* The Bonnie Briar Bush *outside Monksilver School, 1921.*

Left: *Christmas fancy-dress party at Monksilver, 1962. Left to right: Jane Ridler, ?, Freda May, Elizabeth May, Angela Ridler, Nigel Ridler, Hilary Tarr, Margaret Tarr, Andrew Howe, ?, Barbara Howe, Malcolm Blackmore, Philip May, ?, ?, toddler Martin Grellier.*

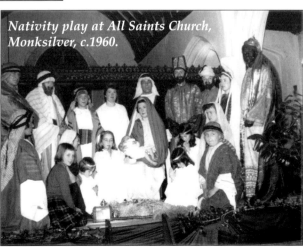

Nativity play at All Saints Church, Monksilver, c.1960.

Monksilver School fancy dress, c.1958. Left to right: *Carol Parsons with Chris Coles, Derek Webb, Angela Young, Shirley Webb, Marilyn Coles.*

❧ *Football* ❧

Right: *Monksilver United Football Club, c.1890.* Left to right, back row: *Edwin Davis (Yarde), Jack Pearse (gamekeeper at Nettlecombe), Marwood Notley, Harry Perkins (Woodford, a printer), Herbert Dyer (butler at Nettlecombe Court), Milo Notley (went to South Africa);* middle: *Marmion Notley (married a Miss Branchflower), Montague Notley, E. Scutt (married Miss Maida Notley), Tom Worth (a groom at Nettlecombe Court);* front: *Sidney Parsons, Edgar Farmer (later to become sub-postmaster at Monksilver and then at Williton).*

Left: *Monksilver Football Team, 1935.* Left to right, back row: *W. Gunney, A. Chave, V. Webber, C. Takle, F. ('Spike') Stevens, W. Hayes, B. Hutchinson;* front: *? Lang, H. Tuckfield (captain), H. Bruford, J. Tuckfield.*

In 2003 Monksilver is without a football team, but has a cricket side who play friendly matches at the Stogumber ground.

Monksilver United Football Club, 1937–8, winners of the Junior Hospital Cup and West Somerset League. Left to right, back: *Reg Ridler, ?, Bill Langdon, H. Norman, B. Trebble, Herbert Tuckfield, F. ('Spike') Stevens, 'Spud' Bowden, Bill May, Charlie May, Walter Moore, ? Bruford, Arthur ('Bungy') May;* front: *George Webber, C. Hayes, R. Norman, H. Bruford, Bert Davis, Albert Chave, Frank Chilcott, Bill Hayes, Jack Tuckfield, Hector Tuckfield, Ernest Bryant.*

❧ *Skittles* ❧

Left: *Notley Arms skittles team, c.1950s. Left to right, back row: S. Dunn, G. Moore, S. Gadd, H. Hooper, E. Moore, E.G. Bryant (landlord); front: J. May, F. ('Spike') Stevens, D. Clarke, G. Langdon, P. Sandford.*

Below: *Herbie Hooper, the Notley's sticker-up for the skittles team, c.1960s.*

Below: *Notley skittles team dinner, c.1950s. Left to right, back: Mollie Clarke, G. Langdon, G. Moore, S. Gadd, H. Hooper, Nancy Bryant, F. ('Spike') Stevens; front: D. Clarke, S. Dunn, E. Moore, P. Sandford, J. May, E.G. Bryant (landlord).*

Bottom left: *The Notley Knockers ladies' skittles team, 2002–3. Left to right, back row: Janice Weetch, Carole Price, Wendy Symes, Lucy Croxton; front: Marion Sear, Jill Sellick, Sarah Matravers.*

Below: *English skittles are taking a back seat to French boules at the Notley in 2003! Left to right: Fred Sheppard, Mike Browning, David Henderson, Tom Lomas.*

❧ *Extracts from Monksilver CE School Log-books, 1875–1953* ❧

The following extracts make fascinating reading and reflect wider social changes. No names have been mentioned here where embarrassment might be caused, and only initials have been inserted in certain places. The log-books are kept at the Somerset Record Office at Taunton. Owing to the 50-year rule, we are unable to publish further extracts, but from 1953 the school remained open for another six years, finally closing on 23 July 1959, at which point pupils transferred to Williton School.

1875

8 June Mr Escott examined the children in religious knowledge and, being satisfied, gave a half-day holiday.

28 June Standard II commenced writing on paper.

5 July A very poor attendance, children employed in gathering whortleberries.

6 Oct. Numbers low – picking acorns.

18 Nov. Mrs Meade King gave a dictation, reading and arithmetic lesson – brought a bag of biscuits for the children.

1 Dec. Several children away through sickness – weather too severe to allow the younger children to be present.

1876

9 Jan. One of the parents sent a message to say she desired her child should not learn the Catechism.

18 Jan. Homework (arithmetic) very poor – several children kept late.

7 April Boy punished for disobedience – ink thrown over wall.

8 August Several children away to carry dinner to the harvest fields.

20 Sept. Geography in Standard II is very backward.

18 Oct. Admitted a boy of 6+ years, not able to say his letters.

27 Oct. Low attendance – children kept home to pick acorns and potatoes.

8 Dec. Examined James Lovell in geography – he could fairly do his continents of Europe, Asia and Africa.

1877

16 Feb. Two girls in Standard I punished for idleness.

6 April Attendance low – children helping their parents in the gardens.

9 April Standard III examined in arithmetic – found two girls were backward in long division.

8 May Two boys were corrected for playing in the street after the bell had gone.

12 June S.A. Watts left school to assist mother. Standard III improved in grammar.

29 June Attendance this week is low, children employed to carry food to their parents in the hayfields.

27 Nov. A boy in Standard III has been without a copy book for two months, his mother refusing to pay 2d for one.

1878

7 Jan. Re-opened school after two weeks vacation, between 40/50 attended. Children not backward in work, but their behaviour is rude and disorderly.

11 Jan. Improvement in order, but in several cases obedience had to be enforced by corporal punishment.

18 Jan. One boy would not submit to punishment, being prompted by his mother.

15 March Many boys attending irregularly as they are required to help with the planting of potatoes.

17 May Two boys punished for using bad language and one for breaking a window through carelessness.

9 Sept. James Holbrook took charge of the school after the four weeks holiday.

22 Nov. Several older children keeping birds this week for the farmers. Average attendance for the week 44 out of 52.

13 Dec. Snow on the ground nearly all week, attendance low, average 39.

1879

6 Jan. Old Christmas Day – attendance very small, it being a general holiday in the neighbourhood.

10 Jan. School almost empty this week due to weather being so severe.

2 May Eight Standard I and II boys played truant yesterday afternoon fox hunting – punished them this morning.

1880

9 Jan. Weather severe, average attendance 40. The Rector reprimanded the older boys for bad behaviour out of school in the village.

16 Jan. School almost empty because of snow.

2 July Government Report: 'I am sorry not to be able to report more favourably of this school. The sums are throughout weak and class subjects do not earn the grant. There is a scarcity of reading books... No grant can be paid the school, being under an uncertificated teacher all year.'

16 Aug. Mr Francis Gilbert Mills now in charge.

3 Sept. Average 25 only. The children are far from encouraging, Standard I not knowing their letters and Standard III failed entirely with the four-times table.

15 Oct. James Lovell has been engaged by the Managers as monitor.

12 Nov. Older boys punished for throwing stones.

10 Dec. Alfred Parsons has a very slight attack of scarlet fever, Mr King ordered school to be closed immediately.

1881

14 Jan. Heavy snow during the week kept the children away.

18 Jan. Weather very severe – school nearly empty.

19 Jan. Impossible for children to attend school, the snow being five feet deep.

28 Jan. The average very low. The beginning of the week the lanes were impassable and when the thaw set in slush prevented many attending.

11 March The treasurer (M. Cox) has ordered more coal for school, 15 cwts. used since Christmas; it is not to be left as usual at School House, but to be taken to the 'The Grange'. A woman is employed to carry in the coal every morning.

5 April S.T. Talbot commenced duties as master of this school.

29 Sept. Frank, Albert and Walter Criddle left the school as they are moving to another parish.

7 Nov. Mrs Lovell's engagement as sewing mistress ends today.

9 Nov. Mrs Branchflower commences duties as sewing mistress and Frank Watts appointed as monitor.

14 Nov. James Lovell's engagement as monitor ends today.

1882 During March several children – Annie Calloway, Sarah A. Proll, Annie Salter, Louisa Routley, John Stanbury and Caroline and Ellen Bennett were admitted to the school.

18 Dec. William Arthur Ward Turner, from Longsight Mixed School, Manchester, took charge of the school.

26 Dec. Mrs Turner appointed monitor.

1883

6 Feb. Shrove Tuesday – attendance only moderate, several staying away to go to the Squire's for pancakes.

12 March Many children away as their parents wanted them to help carry firewood home, M. Notley, Esq., having given them leave to carry away as much as they can in a fortnight.

1884

21 March Received the results of the Ellsworth examinations – Emma Lovell in Standard VI obtained £2.10s.0d. This is the first time the school has been successful. Mary Lane also passed.

6 May Punished three pupils for throwing stones at a poor old man.

24 July Diocesan Prize list – Emma Lovell, a scholar under 14 years of age, having obtained a prize. Only 23 passed in her division.

1 Dec. A boy of eight admitted to school

but was unable to say his two-times table or the alphabet. Alfred Parsons left to work for the Squire.

1885

25 March   Emma Lovell received £2.10s.0d. for the Ellsworth Exhibition.

27 March   Emma Lovell received £2.10s.0d. for the Ellsworth Examination. This is the second time she had received it.

29 June   The Rector wanted to know the boy who stole flowers from the graves. Having found out who it was, I was told to give him a good beating.

17 July   Mr William Turner's last day at school, having been appointed to a school in Yorkshire.

27 July   Mr Arthur Laycock took charge of this school today. Emma Lovell as monitor.

8 Dec.   William and James Hall have measles and several others are unwell.

1886

11 Jan.   The school was closed for three weeks because of the measles epidemic.

5 March   H. Hole received a Prayer Book because he gained the greatest number of marks during the week. The children take great interest in the marks and try hard for the prize.

9 March   Shrove Tuesday – It is the custom to go to houses begging buns, so half-day holiday was allowed.

19 March   Henry Parsons obtained the most number of marks and obtained the prize.

3 July   Copy of Government Report: 'There is a most gratifying change for the better in the tone, discipline and attainments of the school. Indeed the acquirement, though not yet positively good, show so great an advance that I have no hesitation in recommending the Merit Grant of Good. The writing is not yet what it might be owing to scholars having got in the habit of holding their pens wrongly and the first standard are at the disadvantage of writing without desks... There is no urinal in connection with the boys' offices. This omission should be at once supplied. The infants are fairly well taught.' Total grant £51.18s.6d.

1887

30 March   Emma Lovell, the monitress, left for a better position.

5 July   Government Report: Mr Laycock has suffered seriously from illness during the year and has therefore been at great disadvantage. In spite, however, of this drawback his scholars have passed a credible examination in the elementary subjects and have done fairly well in English and geography... The organisation and discipline are fairly good. Mr Laycock will receive his certificate in due course. Grant £47.5s.9d.

26 July   Poor attendance owing to Minehead Races.

29 Nov.   Two children have had accidents –

Alice Stevens bitten by dog and Bertie Bennett broke his leg.

1889

26 April   Received school fees of five children paid for by guardians.

10 May   Girl in Standard IV very backward, have taken great pains with her but she makes no progress. She was one of the girls suspected of copying last year.

11 June   The infants having had a lesson on 'A Blacksmith's Shop' went to the smith's in the village, who kindly showed them the different tools and made a horseshoe.

11 July   Government Report: The Merit of Good is recommended on the grounds of the great improvement exhibited, but much needs doing with reading and spelling. The order and discipline have much improved... the infant class taught by Mrs Laycock show most improvement. The managers would be well advised in securing her as a permanent teacher.

16 Aug.   School treat was held on Rectory lawn. Prizes of books or toys were given for good attendance and good work.

30 Oct.   Mumps have broken out again. School closed till 11 Nov.

1890

31 Jan.   Eight or nine children away sick, two seem to be suffering from scarlet fever – their brothers and sister have been sent home to prevent the spread of the illness.

24 March   Harvey Hole gained £2.10s.0d. from the Ellsworth Exhibition examination. He is in Standard V and only ten years old.

1 April   The only boy in Standard VI has left this school and gone to Stogumber. His parents are jealous that a younger boy than himself should win the Ellsworth examination and so have taken him away.

28 July   The three Misses Notley helped with the sewing lesson.

17 Sept.   The school re-opened. Farmers have not finished harvest and no gleaning until this week – attendance low. The annual treat was given at the Rectory. Prizes given to children attending more than 400 times during the year.

20 Oct.   Mrs Meade King and Misses Clara, Minnie and Maida Notley superintended the sewing.

7 Nov.   Bad attendance – children picking acorns blown down by the storm.

1891

13 March   Snow which commenced to fall on Monday, had reached such a height on Tuesday morning that school was closed until the roads were more passable.

3 July   Have commenced to teach singing by note by the Tonic Sol-fa method.

13 July   Haymaking has commenced and several boys away, some of them having not passed Standard IV. They are working for Mr Hawkins, one of the managers.

14 July   Mrs Laycock went to Sampford Brett School in order to see the musical drill there.

27 July   Misses Clara and Minnie Notley attended the sewing lesson. The latter kindly played the accompaniments to the first two exercises of the new musical drill, which the children are learning.

7 Dec.   Very stormy morning, only 34 children. The very wet weather makes the school very uncomfortable for teachers and scholars.

11 Dec.   Last evening gales blew down a large tree in the Rectory garden, the top of it fell across the offices breaking the roof. The wooden cross on the school was also blown off.

1892

18 Feb.   Snowstorm this morning and none of the children from a distance at school.

1 March   Attendance had dropped so much, Mrs Laycock has sent in her resignation.

4 April   Mr Laycock gave a month's notice to terminate his engagement here.

19 Sept.   Mr H. O'Key starts master's duties today.

3 Oct.   Several children detained after school hours for excessive indolence and noisy conduct.

1893

31 Jan.   The Revd W. Meade King took the Scripture lesson as usual.

24 April   Another large piece of plaster fell from the ceiling – the teacher and several children narrowly escaped.

16 July   This being the day of the Royal Wedding, the children had a holiday.

11 July   Mr Hawkins complained of three from the school going into his orchard. They were kept in for half-hour as punishment.

2 Oct.   The Revd W.T.P. Meade King visited the school in the afternoon and informed me and the children assembled that no corporal punishment, in any form, should be administered, and children were to inform him at once if any thing of the sort took place.

9 Oct.   The Revd Meade King visited this morning and cautioned the children severely about taking nuts into the church, if it occurs again they are to be punished.

1894

28 March   In consequence of Miss Notley's wedding, the children had a holiday.

6 June   The festival of the 'Monksilver Friendly Society' was held in the village today – the children had a holiday.

15 June   Two boys came into school in the afternoon at 2.15 and made a paltry excuse about being sent for some cider.

1895

29 Jan.   Roads very bad with snow. Boy punished slightly for playing with the fire.

5 June   Mr H.L. Okey resigned his post through ill-health. The school is closed for five weeks.

9 July Mr F.J. Salter commenced duties of chief master.

13 Sept. The dictation by Standard III (with two exceptions) was disgracefully written. One boy did not know how to spell 'us' and nearly all could not spell 'tin' and 'coal'.

20 Sept. To try to improve dictation I gave Standards III, IV and V spellings to prepare at home. Five children absent themselves on Tuesday last to witness the marriage of Mr E. Scutt and Miss Maida Notley.

6 Dec. Children away to gather sticks or when their parents are killing a pig.

13 Dec. Gave Standard III, IV and V examination – results exceeded expectations.

1896

24 Jan. Average attendance 21 out of 28 on the books. The Rector is still indisposed and prevented from visiting the school as usual. As neither of the other Managers attend, nothing can be done to improve the attendance.

27 March Standard III and upwards given two examinations – the results are good in both arithmetic and writing.

9 Sept. Revd W.T.P. Meade King died, (correspondent for the school).

19 Oct. Entered infant Annie Moore, aged three years, yesterday.

4 Dec. The new Rector, the Revd Norman King, visited today.

24 Dec. Revd King attended school and each child had two oranges given it by one of the sons of the Rector.

1897

22 Jan. Attendance poor owing to cold weather and the parents say that the schoolroom is very cold and draughty. One window and front door need repair but there is no school funds.

8 March Wind so boisterous that trees, slates and tiles have been blown about to render it too dangerous for grown people to be about, so children were kept in their homes.

18 June The school was dismissed on Friday until 28ʰ in honour of the Queen's Diamond Jubilee.

29 Nov. George Welch now in charge. Amelia Welch sewing mistress.

1898

18 Jan. Requirement of the Education Department – no scholar is to leave school until he or she has attained the age of 13 years no matter what standard may have been passed.

2 May Mr Simon Shepherd, of Rowdon Farm, having been appointed as Churchwarden, is thereby a recognised manager of the school.

19 Sept. Florence and Bessie Bryant, from Colton, admitted.

23 Dec. Just before close of school Revd King came in and gave each child present (26) an orange.

1899

13 Jan. Owing to the wet, children from Colton and Woodford have not attended.

17 April Edward Hall left school to become hall-boy at Combe Sydenham.

5 July H.M. Inspector's Report: The tone of the school is very pleasing and the children take much interest in their work. Among the younger children Mr Welch's careful teaching is bearing fruit, but in the upper part of the school, owing to neglect in the past, cases of individual failures are rather numerous. The ventilation should be improved.

18 July Annual treat at the Rectory.

28 July Small attendance as children have gone picking whortleberries.

8 Sept. Revd King, who is leaving Monksilver for Yorkshire, introduced his successor, the Revd H. Robinson.

15 Sept. The Rector kindly gave apples to the 19 children present this morning.

1900

4 Jan. Miss Notley visited the school this afternoon and gave the children an orange and showed them some mechanical toys.

23 Feb. The Rector showed the children some items placed under a microscope.

7 May General Report: I was glad to find a distinct improvement in this little school. The children's interest in their work and in the upper group answered very credibly. It would be well to try to give a little more attention to the infants and the written work.

4 Dec. School closed today until Monday, 31 Dec., on account of measles and a fatal case of diphtheria.

1901

13 Feb. Dr Killick, Medical Officer of Health for the district, visited for the purpose of examining the closets.

8 May General Report: The improvement in this school under Mr Welch is very marked and calls for commendation. The children have been instructed with care and intelligence.

25 May Mr Welch died today after three days illness – the result of a seizure while gardening.

1 July Mr James Lovell took temporary charge of the school.

25 July Sports at Stogumber – only three in school.

1902

26 June School closed for the Coronation of Edward VII. Children's tea on Friday, each child presented with a book King Edward's Realm.

25 July Poor attendance, bigger boys working with their fathers in the turnip fields.

1903

5 Jan. Re-commenced school – 15 present. Alice Burnett and Herbert Hall in Standard VII won the books.

5 March Admitted John Watts.

3 April Short of coal and still very chilly in school.

1 May Alfred Calloway and Herbert Hall examined and passed in the 3Rs.

29 June A girl in some quarrel had thrown a stone and hit an older girl.

14 July William and Elizabeth Calloway, from Colton, aged nine and eight, admitted.

29 July James and Evelyn Rexworthy and Fred Yendle left.

30 July Mr Montague Notley visited and looked at attendance.

6 Oct. Admitted Charles and Ernest Sully.

1904

26 Feb. Had assistance of girl each morning this week. There are three grades in the infants class and all work is severely handicapped in efforts to keep these at suitable work.

28 March Admitted Lucy Thorn, 11 years, into Standard III.

18 April Some children away since last Oct. for the want of boots.

8 July One boy cannot read words of two letters.

3 Oct. Admitted Florence Watts, infant.

3 Nov. Some boys still unable to say their letters.

29 Nov. A very frosty morning. At playtime the children went for a half-mile run.

17 Dec. From Revd Robinson: The CEC could not increase master's salary or pay salary to sewing mistress (£58 present salary inclusive of sewing mistress – no house).

1905

13 Jan. Very cold, children arranged near the fire. Frank Calloway brought in a dormouse and nest. After warmth of the school had awakened it, it was put in the shrubs.

4 April Revd Robinson showed the children some stereoscopic views of scenery in connection with their geography and left a pictorial magazine for each child.

8 May Florence Moore, three years and ten months, Hilda Thorne, six years, first attendance at any school.

26 July Sports at Stogumber, only eight present in afternoon.

4 Sept. Recommenced, 22 present. Two admitted – Winifred and Mildred Williams.

6 Oct. Better attendance this week, but two slates broken. Class II did arithmetic on paper for first time. Children at a distance (Birchhanger ½ mile, Colton 2 miles, Colton Pits 2½ miles) coming late at morning assembly and missing great part of Scripture lesson.

13 Oct. Revd Robinson presented prizes to the scholars who made the CC required number of attendances: F. Calloway (VI), Roland Hole (IV), John Watts (I), C. Sully and R. Sully (Infants).

3 Nov. Two boys have asked to be

permitted to leave at 3.50 pm to fetch cows for milking by daylight. Allowed to go usually.

13 Nov. The two fresh girls can neither read, write, spell or do sums and have no idea of grammar, history or geography, but came from town schools.

1906

4 May The Revd H. Robinson died last night – all day the children have been silent and saddened.

14 June Florence Moore admitted.

25 Sept. Admitted Dorothy Hole, three years.

22 Oct. Three girls very backward, having lived very far from a school, and all use their left hand.

14 Dec. The new Rector, the Revd F.G. Chorley, arrived this week.

1907

17 July School not opened this afternoon – sports at Stogumber and children were all going.

4 August School not opened. Bank holiday sports at Watchet.

7 Oct. Admitted Percy Potter (5).

1908

20 March Deer hunting in neighbourhood – big boys away in afternoon.

18 Dec. Afternoon school commenced 20 minutes late owing to an error in the time – watch had stopped!

1909

11 Jan. Miss Bertha Brooke appointed by the managers as headmistress.

1 March Miss Gladys Hoddinott appointed by the managers as monitress.

5 March The members of the choir, Arthur Snell, Roland Hole, William Langdon, James Watts and Bessie Calloway, were withdrawn from afternoon school in order to take part in a funeral service.

1 Sept. Started a 'penny library' in the school.

11 Nov. M.M. found to be suffering from ringworm – was told to remain at home until cured.

1910

10 Jan. School opened with an attendance of 24 (31 on roll). Maurice Barker admitted.

8 Feb. School commenced this morning 20 minutes late owing to the stopping of the school clock and the breaking of the headmistress's watch.

22 March The school closed two days earlier than intended owing to telegram summoning headmistress home. Gladys Hoddinott left the school.

5 April School re-opened with an attendance of 25 (roll is 30). Hilda Hole began her duties as monitress.

30 Sept. Hilda Hole left the school. No other monitress has as yet been appointed.

25 Nov. Attendance worse this week owing to inclement weather. Gilbert Watts away all

week owing to bad scald on leg.

1911

31 Jan. W.L. caned today for throwing peas in school and denying it – six strokes on each hand were given.

26 June The school re-opened after the Coronation holiday with an attendance of 26 (two absent)

7 July This week the attendance has been poor owing to haymaking and whortleberry picking. Irene Moore, Delia Snell, Lily Calloway and Mary Bartraham were picking whortleberries.

28 July A half holiday was given in the afternoon for the Day and Sunday School treat to Blue Anchor.

28 Aug. The school re-opened with a roll of 25. Wilfrid Quartley left to go to Queen's College, Taunton. Bessie Calloway began her duties as monitress.

1912

4 March Miss Hallett took temporary charge of the school – found the children in a most backward state and very lax in their behaviour.

19 March Have taken a lesson with all on 'Good Manners'.

2 April Took drill in the road this afternoon.

3 April Miss Hallett's duties as temporary mistress of the school terminates.

22 April I, Millicent Williams, take charge of this school from this date.

6 Dec. Half a ton of coal supplied to the school today.

1913

17 Jan. One child has been away all the week with broken chilblains.

18 Oct. A stove fixed in the upper part of the room where the infants are taught.

1914

25 May Mrs and Miss Shaw visited the school in the afternoon distributing sweets to

the children as they were dismissed at four.

23 July In the afternoon the school was closed and the children were taken to Blue Anchor for their annual summer treat.

27 Nov. The C. school nurse visited the school and examined three children, afterwards asking the head teacher to allow them to sit in a desk by themselves on account of their unclean state.

1915 Copy of report made by HM Inspector after visit on 3 March: 'The heating is still defective; the new stove is frequently out of order and cannot be used; records show that during Jan. and Feb. the average temperature of the schoolroom was only 43 degrees Fahrenheit. The fireplace should at once be repaired; the loose brickwork and heavy stone shelf are in a dangerous condition. The school premises are badly in need of painting and decorating. The seats in the offices should be scrubbed more frequently. The school has no playground; the children play and drill in the public road...'.

3 August The Revd H. Gardner-McTaggart visited the school in the morning.

29 Nov. I have this morning commenced duties as head teacher of this school – E. Clements.

1916

21 Jan. Bessie Calloway resigned duties as monitress.

24 Jan. Nellie Watts, aged 14, commenced duties as monitress.

17 April Admitted Elsie Edith Parsons, aged 4 years.

11 Sept. Admitted Ivy Amelia Calloway, aged 5 years.

20 Oct. George and Cecil Bryant have left the village.

1917

16 Nov. Walter Moore, 14, has left school.

26 Nov. Dorothy Hole and Phyllis Ridler, both 14 years of age, have left school.

Monksilver School, c.1920s. Teacher: Miss Bonner.

1918

12 March Received notice this morning that George Moore, aged 12 years, has passed Labour Certificate examination. He is now entitled to leave school.

19 March George Moore, having obtained employment, has left school.

14 June Florence Calloway, Hilda May Watts and Frances Davis at Stogumber for cookery and housewifery classes.

23 Sept. Frances, Herbert and Phyllis Davis left this school to attend private school at Stream.

14 Oct. Cyril James Ridler, aged 5, entered this school.

21 Oct. I am in charge of this school – F.M. Kyte.

1919

31 Jan. Clifford Ridler has been absent for several weeks with a scalded leg.

1920

27 Feb. The Rector and Mrs Gardner-McTaggart visited to distribute prizes. The winners were: Daisy Parsons (good progress in all subjects), Hilda Watts (composition, drawing, history and geography), Reginald Ridler (arithmetic, drawing and manual work), Elsie Watts (monitor's prize and sewing), Messrs. Brooke, Bond & Co. Ltd. gave four prizes in their writing and drawing competition to Reginald Ridler, Hilda Watts, Ralph Parsons and Annie Moore.

1921

26 Sept. Admitted Daisy Coles from Colton.

1922

27 Feb. Only eight children have assembled today owing to severe colds and influenza.

28 Feb. Holiday to celebrate the marriage of Princess Mary.

20 March The stove was out this morning. It was 11 o'clock before we could get it to burn.

13 Nov. Frances Davis has been appointed monitress.

1923

13 June Poor attendance owing to the wet weather, circus and the church choir outing.

2 July I have today commenced duty at this school – A.W. Bonner.

13 Dec. Fifteen children went to Stogumber this morning for dental treatment.

1924

28 Oct. A holiday has been granted tomorrow as the school is being used as a polling station.

1925

5 Jan. School re-opened, 28 on roll. George Richards and Cecil Parsons have been admitted.

21 April Marjorie Kerslake admitted.

1926

10 May Miss Davis has been appointed as supplementary teacher here.

1927

4 April Denis Davis has been admitted this morning. There are now 25 on books.

26 May Daisy May has been admitted.

1928

4 Sept. Marjorie May has been admitted.

Right: *The school with Miss Piper, c.1930s.*

Below: *Monksilver School, 1927. Left to right, back row: Miss Bonner (headmistress), Edward Cheek, Kathleen Davis, Rex Howe, Clifford Hayes, Geoffrey Ridler, Charlie May, Jim Milton, Bill Cheek, ? Somerfield, Arthur Long, Minerva Long, ?; middle: Emily Cheek, Marjorie Kerslake, Florrie May, Amy Kerslake, ?, Olive Davis, Mary Hayes, Joyce Long, Winnie Long, Marjorie Farmer, Evelyn Parsons, Miss Frances Davis (teacher); front: Arthur May, Daisy May, Millie Eames, Sonny Parsons, Denis Davis, Betty Cheek, Peggy Cheek, ?.*

17 Sept. Maurice Quartley has been admitted; 29 on books.

1929

11 Feb. Children have been sent home because of the deep snow.

1 Oct. This school is now a Junior Department. Ten children were transferred to Williton School – Geoffrey Ridler, Clifford Hayes, Charles May, Willie Cheek, Emily Cheek, Patricia Long, Amy Kerslake, Evelyn Parsons, Florence May and Minerva Long. Thirteen juniors remain.

5 Dec. Betty and Peggy Cheek could not come to school this morning because of floods (Higher Coombe Cross).

1930

20 Feb. Sent all the senior books in this school to Nettlecombe (Yarde) School.

31 March School re-opened today after three weeks closure owing to whooping cough.

1 April Admitted George May to school.

4 April Arthur May transferred to Williton School.

10 April Cecil Parsons and Rex Howe have gone to medical centre at Watchet for eye treatment.

1931

7 Jan. School re-opened – there are now 12 children on the registers.

13 March Cecil Parsons sat for scholarship examination today.

1 June School re-opened – Fred Thorn admitted.

1 Sept. Today I began my work here as mistress-in-charge – Florence M. Piper. There are 14 on roll.

1932

3 May Visited the school this morning and all children present for the examination. We all enjoyed ourselves – Phoebe M. Rees.

13 May Nancy and Mollie Bryant were admitted.

4 July Rex Howe has been transferred to Williton. Ruby May has been admitted.

1933

24 Jan. School closed for three weeks – influenza epidemic.

24 Feb. Heavy snow, only seven children in school.

30 June An open day for parents – 50 present. Denis Davis, Philip Blackmore and Daisy May were transferred to Williton School.

20 Nov. Enie Howe and Hazel Potter ill with measles.

1934

8 Jan. Two new children admitted – Queenie Snell (5) and Vera Hooper (7).

11 Jan. We were able to get water in school tap after six months of no water.

17 April Report by Mr A.M. Moore, HM Inspector: 'The present headmistress (Miss F.M. Piper) has done extremely well here. The children are happy, lively and natural, taking interest and pride in their work... The provision of a playground is much appreciated and it is well used for games and physical training.'

4 Sept. Beryl Hooper and Pamela Calloway admitted – roll 18.

1935

7 Jan. School re-opened 16 children present. Roy Kerslake admitted, Vera Hooper is ill.

6 May A holiday. Children's Jubilee procession through the village 10.30 am, sports in the Court Field 2 o'clock, tea in the Assembly Room 5.30 and social at 7.30 pm. A very happy day.

29 Nov. Vera Hooper won the composition prize, Band of Mercy, gaining first prize for 'Rover, the Collie'.

1936

6 Jan. Miss Rosemary Allen has joined the staff as a monitress. Our new Rector, Revd F.S. Strother, looked in to make the acquaintance of the children.

21 Jan. Our beloved King George V passed away at midnight at Sandringham.

28 Jan. No school – funeral of our King in St. George's Chapel, Windsor – R.I.P.

1937

11 Jan. School re-opened. Cecil Potter and George May attend Williton School. Number on books 16.

1 Feb. N. Webb commenced duty...

6 April School re-opened. James Watts admitted.

7 May Children gave a small concert in the evening and from it gained £2.5s.0d. – their contribution towards the playground improvements.

11 May The school was closed for the Coronation holiday (three days) and

Monksilver Junior School, 1937. Left to right, back row: Audrey Kerslake, Mollie Bryant, Vera Hooper, Fred Thorn, Raymond Davis, Peter Quartley, Albert Snell; front: Ruby May, Donald Potter, Beryl Hooper, Queenie Snell, Pamela Calloway, Mary Kerslake, Roy Kerslake.

Whitsuntide holiday (one week).

30 June   Fred Thorn leaves today for Williton Senior School.

31 Aug.   School re-opened today after summer holidays – 14 children from Elworthy and Willett were admitted owing to the closure of Elworthy School. There are now 30 children on the roll. Mrs Davis of Yarde began duty here today as supplementary teacher.

6 Sept.   The playground is now tarmac. Mr. Moore, HMI, advised a screen to be placed between the two classes.

18 Oct.   Kathleen Snell admitted today.

1938

28 March Pamela Hill admitted today.

13 April   Rosemary Allen ended her duties here as monitress.

6 May   A half day holiday because Raymond Davis passed the first part of the Scholarship examination.

13 June   R. Davis has gained scholarship tenable at Minehead School.

17 June   Copy of Diocesan report: 'This is a small but interesting school, well controlled and efficiently taught. The singing was bright and tuneful and the syllabus had been carefully thought out and taken in an interesting way. The infant group under Mrs Davis answered very well; the teacher shows a knowledge of children and she certainly gets the very best out of them. In the upper group the written work was praiseworthy and the children answered very well in all branches of the syllabus. Their eagerness and brightness showed clearly that the teaching had been efficient. The mark for this school is V.G.'

1939

9 Jan.   School re-opened. Barbara Baker and Ruby May left for Williton School. Admitted Kenneth Stephens.

25–26 Jan. Children from Elworthy and Willett not at school – road not safe for bus.

25 May   Afternoon holiday for schools' area sports. Teddy Phillips gained 2nd place for high jump, Don Potter 3rd for long jump, Mary Kerslake 3rd for flat race.

1 July   Donald Potter transferred to Williton Senior School.

31 Aug.   School closed owing to the evacuation of children from urban areas.

11 Sept.   School re-opened – seven London children admitted.

6 Oct.   We now have seven official London evacuees and two private evacuees from Birmingham. Number of children on roll altogether is now 33.

1 Nov.   Five of the evacuees cannot read, although one is eight... and another seven...

1940

8 Jan.   School re-opened. John Creedy and Alan Baker admitted.

19 Jan.   Heavy snow – only three children on bus to school and only 11 present.

7 May   Roland Bragg (from Colton) attended school today – has over two miles to walk and is not yet six years old.

1941

23 May   John Baker and Gordon Snell have passed the scholarship examination. Mrs Davis absent because her husband is very ill.

26 May   Twenty-three evacuees from Bristol...

27 May   Nancy Bryant kindly offered to help in school during Mrs Davis' absence; the Rector also giving part-time help.

3 June   Mrs Davis returned to school.

16 June   The senior boys of the Bristol school party of evacuees have been transferred to Yarde School.

1942

11 May   Austin Phillips has passed the scholarship examinations.

30 June   Betty Milton leaves here today in order to attend Williton Senior School. I finish my duties as head teacher here today – N. Webb.

1 Oct.   Today I assumed duties of headmistress – F.M. Piper.

1943

14 April   The headmistress was absent this afternoon to attend, with the Guides, Mrs Wolseley's funeral.

17 May   Mollie Irene Daw gained a 'free place' at Bishops Fox's Girls' School.

18 Oct.   Twenty children had dinners in school today – sent from the Wiveliscombe canteen.

Monksilver School, 1946. Left to right, back row: *Shirley Webber, Derek Watts, Heather Potter, Louise Ford, Brian Somerfield;* middle: *Roger Ling, Janet Ling, Rita Hayes, Ernie Nicholls, Anthony Blackmore;* front: *Clifford Hill, Valerie Stevens, Betty Baker.*

9 Nov.   Today, as there was no fires in school, I took the children out to gather sticks as the school was so cold. – F.M. Piper.

1944

3 Aug.   Broke up for a month's holiday. We have had no water in school for a fortnight. The boys carried water.

4 Sept.   Re-opened school. Still no water.

20 Oct.   School closed. Water trickling through pipes after torrential rains.

1945

8 Jan.   Re-opened school. Snow and ice prevent children from Elworthy being present – seven children here.

10 April   The Nettlecombe-Yarde School has been closed and the seven children have been admitted here. There are 28 children on... roll.

10–11 May Tuesday and Wednesday were VE days so the school was closed.

5 Sept.   VJ Days added to the five weeks' holiday. Twenty-one children present – mumps in the village. John Creedy and Derek Davis gained scholarships for Taunton School and Huish Grammar School respectively.

1946

17 May   Alan Baker and Desmond White taking scholarship examination today – the rest of the school not in attendance.

29 May   Bird and Tree Festival. Garnet Wolseley, Esq., gave a delightful talk on the birds and trees of the district. Miss Jane Wolseley presented prizes to: Derek Davis, Sorrel Corfield, Alan Baker, John Creedy, Desmond White, Brian Somerfield, Derek Watts, Ernest Nicholls and Jean Routley.

1947

30 Jan.   No children have arrived – a blizzard is blowing and snow blocking the roadway.

10 Feb.   The last week nine children – pipes frozen. School now closed.

10 March The thaw has commenced, we have re-opened school but with only nine children. All pipes are still frozen.

20 Nov.   Princess Elizabeth was married to Lt. Philip Mountbatten, Duke of Edinburgh – a whole day's holiday.

1948

12 May   Rita Hayes and Louisa Ford have passed the scholarship examination for Minehead Grammar School and Heather Potter for Bishops Fox's School, Taunton.

20 July   Prize Day. Resume: This year has been a very good one! We came first in the Junior section of the Bird and Tree Shield Competition. The best essays written in Somerset in this section were those of Louisa Ford and Ernest Nicholls, who won medals. Heather Potter came first in painting in the local National Savings posters, Rita Hayes was runner-up for the Queen of the District for posture and speech.

9 Sept.   Anthony Blackmore, Michael Hill, Tom Welch have been admitted into the top class.

Monksilver School, c.1947. Left to right, back row: *Clifford Hill, Derek Watts, Brian Somerfield, Mrs Davis, Ernie Nicholls, Ken Tudor, Brian Watts;* front: *Hubert Hill, Michael Hill, Anthony Blackmore, Clifford Hill, Rodney Somerfield.*

Below: *Monksilver School, 1957.* Left to right, back row: *Roger Grellier, Robert Moore, Peter Ridler, Brian Stevens, Gerald May, William Gulliford;* third: *Elizabeth Ansell, ?, Mary Dutton, Freda May, Sandra Moore, Barbara Symes, Angela Young, ?, Jennifer Dymond, ?;* second: *Angela Ridler, Mary Hall, Pam Blackmore, Carol Stark, Susan Grellier, Anne Turner, Elizabeth May;* front: *Malcolm Blackmore, Paul Grellier, George Hall, Philip May, Jonathan Turner.*

Bottom: *Monksilver School, which closed in 1959.*

Below: *Monksilver School, c.1956.* Left to right, back row: *George Hall, Peter Ridler, Carol Stark, Pam Blackmore, Brian Stevens, Richard Taylor, Robert Moore, William Gulliford, Philip May;* middle: *Mary Hall, Angela Young, Elizabeth May, Angela Ridler, Mary Dutton, Freda May, Sandra Moore;* front: *Jonathan Turner, Jennifer Dymond, William Ansell, ? Fox-Smith, A. Gulliford, ?, Barbara Symes.*

1 Oct. Mrs Davis has left today after many years of teaching in Somerset. The children are collecting to give her a present.

1949

4 March No fires, temperature 40 degrees – two oil stoves, but not much heat.

23 May All children present – 19 on roll.

13 June I resumed duties today – Florence M. Piper.

12 Dec. Today six children are present – all the others are down with mumps.

1950

4 Sept. Induction of new Rector: Revd R.P. Wickens. A half-day's holiday was given.

19 Dec. This is the last day of school for me, I really retire today from the teaching profession – 17 years in Africa and 15 in England – Florence M. Piper.

1951

30 Jan. Admitted two new children, Irene and Kathleen Brown. Total of 25 on registers, all under one teacher.

3 Sept. Today I commenced my duties as headmistress of this school – Mrs M.R. Chipp. There are only 18 on roll and all are present. One child admitted – Wendy Gadd.

19 Dec. School concert at 7 pm – a good attendance... collection amounted to £1.7s.6d.

1952

7 Jan. School re-opened, 20 out of 21 present. Three infants admitted – Peter Ridler, Brian Stevens and Carol Stark.

6 Feb. Our beloved King George VI died peacefully at Sandringham.

28 April School re-opened after Easter – 23 out of 23 present. Admitted Robert Moore (infant) and Barrie Eardley (junior).

1 Sept. School re-opened after mid-summer holidays – 21 children on roll. I resumed

work – M.R. Chipp. Tommy Welch, Michael Hill and Margaret Moore transferred to Williton School, Marion Ash admitted.

9 Sept. Admitted Michael Saltmarsh from Elworthy.

1–3 Dec. Many children absent... icy roads.

1953

18 Jan. Admitted Elizabeth May.

3 Feb. Rosemary Fry, Valerie Stevens and Daisy Welch are taking the County Examination.

19 April Today I relinquished my post as headmistress of Monksilver VA School – M.R. Chipp.

20 April Doreen Morse admitted.

4 June School commenced after Whitsun holiday, an extra three days having been given for the Coronation.

31 August Today I, Agnes Mary Rees, began work as headmistress of this school.

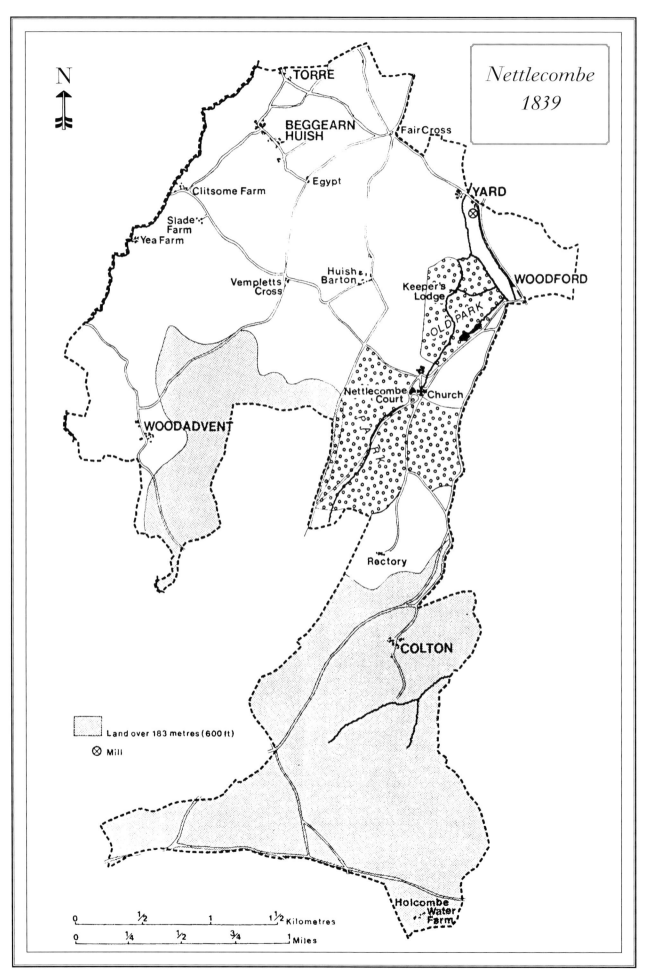

N

Nettlecombe
1839

TORRE

BEGGEARN
HUISH

FairCross

Egypt

YARD

Clitsome Farm

Slade
Farm
Yea Farm

Huish
Barton

Keeper's
Lodge

WOODFORD

Vempletts
Cross

OLD PARK

Nettlecombe
Court

Church

P
A
R
K

WOODADVENT

Rectory

COLTON

Land over 183 metres (600 ft)

⊗ Mill

Holcombe
Water
Farm

0   ½   1   1½ Kilometres

0   ¼   ½   ¾   1 Miles

Three

Nettlecombe

The parish of Nettlecombe lies within the bounds of the Exmoor National Park, and much of it is above the 152-metre contour, reaching 358 metres on the Brendon ridgeway. Lying mostly on slate, iron ore was mined in the parish during the nineteenth century, and there were quarries at Woodadvent, Beggearn Huish, Colton, Woodford, Yarde, Holcombe Water and Torre.

Proceeding northwards along the valley road from Monksilver for about a mile one arrives at a left turning at Woodford which leads to the sixteenth-century mansion of Nettlecombe Court and the adjacent Parish Church of St Mary. Even today there is a certain ambience surrounding Nettlecombe, and as one views the splendour of the surroundings it is easy to visualise the historic scenes of the past.

Nettlecombe Court and Parish Church, c.1890.

The actual village near the church and manor-house was removed when landscaped improvements were made to the Park in the late 1700s. During the 1800s the village disappeared completely and Woodford was built instead to house the local workers, the Court and estate being the main source of employment; Yarde and Torre also grew when Nettlecombe village was removed.

The lovely Church of the Blessed Virgin Mary, so dedicated by 1440, was built by the lords of the manor of Nettlecombe as their own and for the use of their retainers. The history of the building is, naturally, very much tied up with that of the Court and of the Ralegh and Trevelyan families, who owned it and lived there; some of the incumbents were members of these families. It is thought that a church had been built at Nettlecombe by the late 1100s, but one was certainly there in 1216, although the list of incumbents does not begin until 1297. The church is now part of the Quantock Towers Benefice.

Built mainly of local red sandstone, the church comprises a chancel (flanked by a chapel to the north and the organ chamber to the south), a clerestoried nave (flanked by north and south aisles), a north porch, and a tower over the west door. There is no south door and, on this side, two tomb recesses project beyond the south wall into the churchyard.

The building was restored around 1820 and, more extensively, between 1858 and 1870. In the early 1930s an electricity supply was provided, but the most striking visible alteration to the church during the last century must be the east window. Made by Martin Travers in 1935, it was given in memory of Sir Walter John Trevelyan (1866–1931), the last of the Trevelyan baronets to live at the Court, and of his younger daughter, Urith (1906–29). Portrayed are the Court and church, and the Christ Child holding a scroll. The heraldry on the left side depicts the arms of Sir Walter and the white demi-horse rising from the waves denoting Trevelyan, whilst on the right are the golden coins for his wife, Alice (née Money), and the lozenge-shaped Trevelyan badge. The letters UT are for Urith.

In the western recess the two figures are said to be those of Sir John de Ralegh and his first wife Maud. She may have died in 1360, and he remarried in 1372. His effigy is 2.1m (7ft) long, although it is not known whether he was really that tall. The bronze figure of the Virgin Mary and Child on the north wall (made by Ernest Gillick in 1945) is a memorial to Joan Alys Wolseley (1904–43), who was the last owner of Nettlecombe Court to have borne the name Trevelyan.

The church clock is fitted with a Graham-type escapement that dates it after about 1775. The minutes of the annual parochial church meeting held in March 1954 record that the retiring churchwarden, Mr Macauley, offered to take the clock down and repair it free of charge. No record was made of what was wrong with it, but money was evidently

❦ *Church of the* ❦
Blessed Virgin Mary

Right and below: *Church parade at Nettlecombe, c.1920.*

Bottom left: *Some of the 128 exhibits on show at the Crib Festival in January 2003 at St Mary's Church, Nettlecombe. It was the second to be held there, being the idea of the priest-in-charge, the Revd Elfrida Savigear, who asked parishioners of the Quantock Towers Benefice to lend their crib sets for the display. It was all lit by candles and night-lights and was particularly magical. The sets came from all over the world, including Peru, Spain, Bangladesh and Nigeria. There was organ music and handbell ringing as well as a visit from the Bishop of Bath and Wells, the Rt Revd Peter Price.*

Left: *Nettlecombe Church tower restoration, c.1930s.*

Below: *The ancient chalice and paten of Nettlecombe Parish Church.*

Below: *St Mary's Church, Nettlecombe, seen from the north-east; the Trevelyan Chapel is to the left, 2002.*

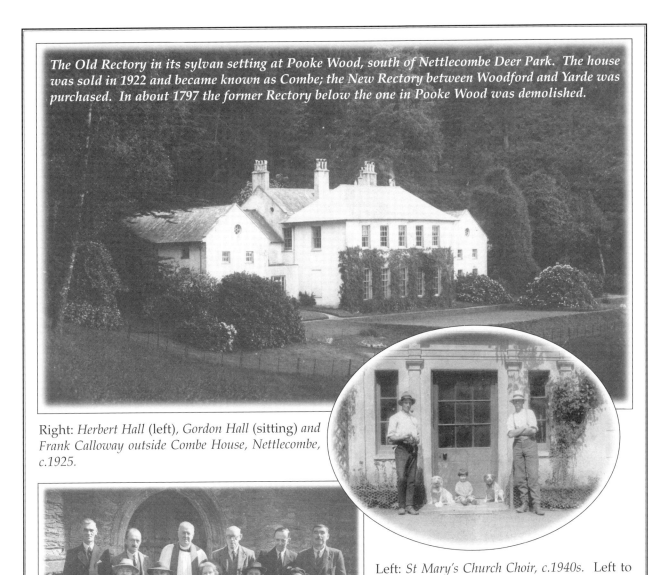

The Old Rectory in its sylvan setting at Pooke Wood, south of Nettlecombe Deer Park. The house was sold in 1922 and became known as Combe; the New Rectory between Woodford and Yarde was purchased. In about 1797 the former Rectory below the one in Pooke Wood was demolished.

Right: *Herbert Hall (left), Gordon Hall (sitting) and Frank Calloway outside Combe House, Nettlecombe, c.1925.*

Left: *St Mary's Church Choir, c.1940s.* Left to right, back row: *J. Routley, Jack Davis, Revd F.B. Corfield, N.B. Macauley, W. Hole, A. Burnett;* middle: *Miss A. Tooze, Miss Bond (organist), Miss P. Rees, Mrs M. Hayes, Mrs N. Tuckfield;* front: *Tom Somerfield, Basil Jones.*

Right: *The third Nettlecombe Rectory, situated between Woodford and Yarde, as it was in c.1905 when it was a private house. It was bought as a Rectory in the early 1920s, but was sold in 1968 when the last resident rector left. It is now a private house again.*

Nettlecombe Cricket Team, c.1930s. Left to right, back row: *N.B. Macauley, W. Hayes, ?, Robert Tarr, ?, ?,*
? Willis; front: *?, ?, Harold Davis, Horace Notley, E. Stevens, H. Stevens, A. Burnett;*
seated on ground: *Tom Somerfield.*

required as donations were sought following the 1956 annual meeting. Time waits for no one, but this proved to be an exception as it was not until 1997 that the clock was finally reinstated in full working order! This was under the direction of Mr Arthur Wood.

The Nettlecombe chalice and paten, dated pre-Reformation (1439–79), are the oldest pieces of hallmarked church plate in the country and of priceless value. The design work is of singular beauty and the colours of the enamel in the centre of the paten are still quite brilliant. They were presented to the church by John Trevelyan, who acquired Nettlecombe through his marriage to Elizabeth Whalesborough in 1452. In the troubled times of the Reformation, when the family clung to the old way whilst the church followed the new, 'a medieval chalice' was covertly transferred to John Trevelyan when the chantry chapel was suppressed in 1548. This would account for its presence in the Court, amongst the family silver hidden under the floorboards by Margaret Trevelyan during the Civil War.

The plate was not recovered until the eighteenth century when a maid dropped a valuable thimble between the floorboards and they were taken up. The putative value of the chalice and paten has so increased that they are now kept in the Victoria & Albert Museum and only brought back to Nettlecombe for use on rare occasions.

The Trevelyans owned all estates in the parish by the early-eighteenth century except Beggearn Huish,

which was split into several large freeholds, later known as Clitsome, Torre and Slade. There was also a substantial leasehold farm at Yarde, which was within the Nettlecombe manor. There were five farms over 250 acres in the parish by 1838, all on the Trevelyan estate. In 1821 there were 66 families, of whom 54 were engaged in agriculture, living in 59 houses, and in 1851 there were 68 labourers recorded on nine farms. Less than a third of the land was under the plough by 1976, but the size of the holdings had not changed significantly since the 1830s.

Woodadvent does not appear in the Domesday survey, but in 1284 Robert Avenant held half a fee at Woodadvent; the Avenants probably held the estate in succession to the Wood family. In 1327 it was held by Thomas FitzUrse, who is said to have married a daughter of Robert Avenant. Woodadvent was settled by Thomas FitzUrse on John de Ralegh in 1335 and it reverted to his eldest son, Sir John de Ralegh, and descended with Nettlecombe manor. In 1523 a house at Woodadvent (now listed) was referred to as the manor place, and in 1619 was described as a farm, later being rebuilt in the early 1800s by the second Sir John Trevelyan. Woodadvent Farm consists of 350 acres and the house also accommodates guests.

In 1066 Huish, later Beggearn Huish, was held by Merlesuain and in 1086 by Ralph Pagnell. John de Ralegh held the estate in 1362 and, following further changes in ownership, it was conveyed to Lucy Luttrell in trust for Francis Luttrell, of Dunster, in

1679. In 1682 the manor was mortgaged to Sir William Wyndham and after the death of Francis Luttrell in 1690 it was forfeited to Wyndham, in whose family it descended.

Largely rebuilt and extended northwards in the seventeenth century, Huish Barton is probably in origin a sixteenth-century house. A plaster panel bearing the date 1698 appears over a fireplace, as does the monogram of the Musgraves, who occupied the house for most of the seventeenth century. A barn, probably of the late-seventeenth or early-eighteenth century, is among the adjoining farm buildings.

In 1843 deposits of iron ore were found in the parish at Fair Cross and Beggearn Huish, where a mine was opened. However, mining was concentrated at Colton, where possible eighteenth-century workings were found in the 1860s. The mining rights at Colton pits were leased by the Trevelyans in 1859 in return for a minimum rent of £50 and a charge of 1s. for every ton of ore. In 1865 a new adit was opened by the Ebbw Vale Steel, Iron and Coal Co. The Colton mine was worked on five levels in 1881, but the ore was still carried to Brendon Hill by horse and cart. In 1882 the mines were closed, but they were reopened in 1907 by the Somerset Mineral Syndicate. Following this, a light railway was constructed to carry ore to the mineral railway at Brendon Hill. To carry ore from Galloping Bottom up the new line an incline with boiler and winding engine was installed; a steam pump enabled working at lower levels. In 1908 over 2,000 tons of ore were mined, but a slump in the steel industry led to the mines being closed in 1909.

In his book, *Exmoor in Wartime*, Jack Hurley states that during the Second World War the area along the Watchet–Wiveliscombe road appeared to be something of a bomb path. On 23 August 1940 no less than 17 bombs fell around Nettlecombe. Open ground received every one and only slight damage occurred, but later in the year the blast of a parachute bomb did a great deal of damage at and around the Old Rectory (now Combe House). In April 1941 incendiary bombs destroyed stables and outbuildings on Colton Farm, damaging Combe House so severely that the occupants had to be evacuated. Colton farmhouse suffered in the same incident. It was not then known that an unexploded parachute mine was lying in a nearby wood; nine days later it exploded and Colton farmhouse was knocked about once again.

The population of the parish reached a peak of 372 in 1821, but fell to 259 in 1891, caused possibly by the closure of the iron ore mines. In 1981 the population stood at 166, but by 2001 it had risen to some 240.

In 1836 Nettlecombe became part of the Williton Poor Law Union and from 1894 was in the Williton Rural Ristrict. It has been part of the West Somerset District since 1974 and has a Parish Council.

Above: *Mr Tarr* (left) *and Miss 'I.C.E. Cream' (Revd Fred Corfield) at Nettlecombe Court, c.1930s.*

Left: *Teaching and domestic staff of St Audries Junior School at Nettlecombe Court, c.1960. Left to right, back row: Cyril Triggol, Ada Richards, ?, Mrs Andrews, ?, Mr Covey; front: ?, Amy May, Agnes Potter, Mrs Covey, Gladys Bellamy, Beattie Taylor, ?.*

Right: *1st Nettlecombe Company Girl Guides, c.1920s. Left to right, back row: Lt Frances Davis, Muriel Stevens, J. Long, P. Davis, Capt Joan Trevelyan, V. Aplin, V. Davis, K. Davis, M. Long; front: E. Davis (with Lassie), L. Bryant, B. Somerfield.*

❧ *Outlying Farms* ❧

Top left: *Woodadvent, c.1930.*

Above: *Huish Barton Farmhouse.*

Left: *Beggearn Huish Manor, c.1905.*

Below: *Chidgley Farm, 1957.*

Above: *Working horses and men at Nettlecombe in the early 1900s.*

Right: *Thatching spar competition, c.1930s.* Left to right: *Messrs C. Howe, Criddle, C. Duddridge and F. Cheek.*

An Edwardian meet of the Nettlecombe Harriers at Colton.

LOT 12   *(Coloured Pink on Plan No. 1)*

CHIDGLEY FARM

Chidgley

406 a.   2 r.   19 p.

(406.622 Acres—See separate Schedule)

Description	Area	Tenant	Tenancy	Rent per annum £ s. d.
Chidgley Farm	404.032	Mr. A. E. Walker ..	Yearly Michaelmas Agreement dated 1.9.1947	531 0 0
Woodland	2.590	In Hand ..	.. Vacant Possession	—

Outgoings: Tithe Redemption Annuity £48 12s. 1d. (informally apportioned). Land Tax, see Outgoings under General Remarks.

THE CAPITAL DAIRY AND MIXED FARM

is situated to the south of Nettlecombe Park on the public road midway between Fair Cross and Raleigh's Cross. It lies on the edge of the Brendon Hills, and is 5 miles south of Watchet.

THE FARMHOUSE

which stands on a bank just off the road, is reached by a front pathway. It is mainly built of stone with a slated roof. The south-west elevation is protected by galvanised iron sheeting.

The accommodation comprises:

On the Ground Floor: **Entrance Porch; Entrance Hall** with cupboard under stairs; **Sitting Room** with fireplace; **Dining Room** with fireplace; **Kitchen** with Triplex combination range with hot water boiler, cupboard under stairs and store cupboard; **Scullery** with deep sink (h. & c.); **Larder** with slate shelves; and **Coal Store.**

On the First Floor: Approached by stairway from Hall to the Landing: **Six Bedrooms,** two with fireplaces and two with hanging cupboards; **Bathroom** with heated airing cupboard; **Separate W.C.;** and **Apple Room** with fruit racks and outside door, now used for storage.

18

Sale particulars, 1957. Chidgley Farm sold for £6,750.

Outside: Wash-house with copper.   Wood Store.   Store Shed.

Estate Water Supply.   Tenant's own Electric Light to ground floor.   Drainage to pond.

Front Garden with lawns and flower beds.   Kitchen Garden and Orchard opposite.

THE FARM BUILDINGS

There is a main group to the east of the farmhouse and they are mostly built of stone with slated roofs.   There is a Central Yard.   The buildings include: Lean-to **Dairy** with concrete floor; **Three-stall Stable** used as Cowhouse with mangers and hay racks; **Cowhouse for 10** with concrete floor and mangers, hay racks, chain ties and wooden partitions; similar **Cowhouse for 10** on other side of building and having automatic water bowls; **Two lean-to Pigstyes; Hay Loft** and **Chicken House** over cowhouses; **Two Pigstyes; Cowhouse for 7** with mangers, hay racks and feeding passage; **Food Store; Granary** over; **Implement Shed; Garage;** and **Implement Shed.**

On the opposite side of the road are the following buildings round a **Cattle Yard** or **Court** with water trough: Lean-to **Implement Shed;** thatched **Barn; Cattle Shed** with manger and hay rack; **Two Calf Barns; Cattle Shed** with manger; **Tractor Shed; Six-bay Dutch Barn** with galvanised iron roof and end wind shields on steel stanchions; and **Implement Shed.**

In O.S. No. 212 there is a **Cattle Yard** with **Open Cattle Shed.**

TWO COTTAGES

Opposite the farmhouse is a stone and thatched **COTTAGE** containing: **Entrance Hall; Sitting Room** with brick fireplace and cupboard; **Kitchen** with range; **Scullery** with sink (c.) and copper; **Wash-house** with copper; **Two Bedrooms;** and **Two Attic Bedrooms.** *Outside:* Bucket Closet. Fuel Store. Large Garden. *Estate Water Supply.*

Just to the north there is a semi-detached **COTTAGE** built of stone with a thatched roof.   It contains: **Entrance Porch; Living Room** with range; **Sitting Room** with brick fireplace and cupboard under stairs; **Scullery** with deep sink (c.); **Store Room;** and **Four Bedrooms,** one with boxroom. *Outside:* Wash-house with copper. Bucket Closet. Pigstye. Large Garden. *Estate Water Supply.*

THE LAND

much of which is sloping conveniently, surrounds the homestead and is intersected by public roads and tracks which afford good access to most of the fields.   The land lies between about 600 and 1,000 feet above sea level in the Brendon Hills.

NOTES:

Chidgley Estate Water Supply: See Special Condition of Sale No. 18.

Rights of Way: This Lot is sold subject to rights of way for all purposes in favour of (1) Lot 16 between the points F—G and (2) Kingsdown Clump between the points H—I—J—K, all marked on the Sale Plan No. 1.

Drainage Easement: This Lot is sold subject to a drainage easement in favour of the detached Cottage at Sticklepath to drain into a septic tank situated on this Lot.

Drainage Easement: This Lot is sold subject to a drainage easement in favour of Nettlecombe Lodge, which has been sold, to drain into a newly constructed septic tank system situated on this Lot.   See Special Condition of Sale No. 18.

19

Top left: *Cottage No. 1 at Woodford, built in 1852.*

Top right: *The Agent's House, Woodford, 1957.*

Above left: *Court Cottage at Woodford, scene of a triple murder in 1773.*

Centre right: *Eva 'Bessie' Somerfield ready to wield the willow for Nettlecombe WI cricket team.*

Above: *Sidney Bennett, of Woodford, the chauffeur to Lady Trevelyan and a good servant to Garnet Wolseley.*

Right: *Cottages at Woodford, c.1900.*

Woodford

A mile north of Monksilver is the hamlet of Woodford, most of the dwellings of which were at one time inhabited by workers from the nearby Nettlecombe Court and estate. A row of five stone-built terraced cottages were constructed from 1852–65, and the fine building which was Nettlecombe's third Rectory (now a private house) stands further along the road towards Yarde. There are other buildings, including a cottage, originally of the Jacobean period, which lies back off the road. Here in 1773 lived a family of three women – Mrs Elizabeth Conibeer, aged 88, and her two daughters, Ann (45) and Sarah (43). They were eating their lunch on 5 July when death struck them down in a most horrible fashion. Through the open cottage door came a madman who stabbed all three to death, leaving them lying in a pool of blood. An approaching baker's lad heard nothing as he carried his loaves to the now half-open door. He was petrified when he saw the horror inside, and he turned and ran to raise the alarm. Jack Hurley explains in *Murder and Mystery on Exmoor* that the hideous crime was never solved. The Conibeers were buried in Monksilver churchyard, where their headstone is still to be seen *(right)*.

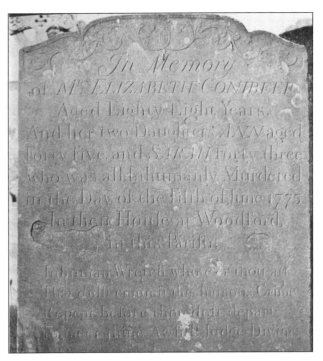

Headstone of the murdered Conibeers in Monksilver church-yard. The inscription includes 'Inhuman wretch, who'er thou art That didst commit this heinous crime, Repent, before thou dost depart To meet thy awful Judge Divine.'

Cottages at Woodford, mid-1920s, and (inset) *Walter 'Jesse' Somerfield, of Woodford* (left), *with his brother Herbert, of Stogumber. Walter was head gardener at the Court for many years and was Tom and Beatie's father.*

Above: *The stream at Yarde, c.1910.*

Right: *Yarde Farm, 1957.*

Below: *Yarde, c.1910.*

Opening of the skittles alley at Yarde, 1950. Left to right, back row: *N.B. Macauley, Wally ('Bungy') Barnes, L. Merson, Norman Fitton, Revd G.M. Hickman, E.G. Bryant;* third row: *Frank Stevens, Bill May, Mr Booth, H. Stevens, Tom Somerfield, Dennis Merson, Harry Jones, Sidney Bennett, Walter Somerfield, Ernest Andrews;* second (seated): *Horace Routley, Stan Stevens, Harold Gregory, Reg Edwards, Bert Parkman, Jack Bryant;* front: *Arthur Antill, Charlie Stevenson, Garnet Wolseley, Jack Davis, Jim Hole.*

Yarde

Situated about half a mile to the north of Woodford is the picturesque hamlet of Yarde, which boasts many historical features and played a prominent part in the educational and social life of the parish. Yarde emerged as a hamlet in the early-fourteenth century, at which time it was known as Yeird, meaning enclosed ground or yard from the Old English geard. Another derivative could be from the heyday of its orchards, the word coming from the Old English wortgeard, literally 'a fruit yard'. The spelling of Yarde has varied down through the centuries, but for the most part the 'e' was omitted. In recent times, however, it most commonly appears with an 'e' at the end. The main road through the hamlet was built in 1820, together with an arch over the river near Yarde Farm, and continues meandering through a beautiful little valley and on up to Elworthy and beyond.

Beer was being sold illegally in the parish in 1658, and in 1661 an alehouse was recorded. An inn at

Yarde was first mentioned in 1736 and was sited by the bridge and stream east of Yarde Farmhouse, but by 1822, following a road alteration, a different building (Yarde Farmhouse) was being used for the inn, although trading under the same name as its predecessor – the Hare and Hounds. It catered for those travelling from Minehead to Taunton and Wiveliscombe, and the story prevails that a small room at the rear of the premises was used to lock up the drunks and rowdies until they sobered up the following morning!

In 1840 a Trevelyan Arms at Yarde was mentioned, but no later record of a public house in the parish has been found. It is said that Sir Walter Calverley Trevelyan (1797–1879), a staunch teetotaller and president of the United Temperance Alliance, had the pub closed and transformed it back to its earlier use as a farmhouse. He built the Temperance Hall at Roadwater in an effort to 'reform' the iron-ore miners and the slate quarry workers living nearby, and he also encouraged temperance meetings in Nettlecombe Park.

Opposite page: *Edward Davis (the Nettlecombe estate blacksmith who had a forge at Yarde) and Mrs Davis, c.1870. They produced six children, five of whom were born in Scott's Cottage, Yarde. The family eventually moved to nearby Yarde House and carried on a smithing business there, employing six hands.*

Above: *The former Blade Mill at Yarde.*

Below: *Yarde Mill House and Water Mill, parts of which are said to date back to the fourteenth century. The mill was a prosperous business, especially from 1840–60 when it supplied the mining community on the Brendon Hills. The building is now a private residence.*

Above: *The large cider press (now used as a dining table) in situ at the Racking House at Yarde.*

Right: *The old water-wheel at Yarde Mill.*

Aerial view of Yarde Farm, c.1955. This was also the site of the second public house at Yarde, the Hare and Hounds.

In 1752 Sir John Trevelyan leased Yarde Farm to yeoman Rob Culliford, of Old Cleeve, for seven years at an annual rent of £50 (excluding the turnip crop). From 1807 until 1829 or later there was a friendly society in Nettlecombe – the Nettlecombe Union and Friendly Society – which met at the Hare and Hounds Inn or at Yarde Mill once a month. Annual feasts were held on Whit Tuesdays, and in 1828 there were 180 members. Then belonging to Nettlecombe manor, the historic Yarde Mill House and adjoining Mill dates back to the fourteenth century, being mentioned in 1374–5. The mill was a prosperous business, especially from 1840–60 when it supplied the iron-ore mining villages on the Brendon Hills. The miller was also a corn, seed and coal merchant in 1872, but milling ceased after 1910. However, the mill, old water-wheel and various stones still survive. A $^1/_{12}$th scale working model of the mill was commissioned by the British Science Museum in conjunction with the Victoria & Albert Museum in the 1970s. The property is now a private residence. Near the mill is Yarde House (originally called Forge House), which was built at the turn of the nineteenth century by the Nettlecombe estate for blacksmith Edward Davis; the house incorporated a smithy and well. The village pump, which is still standing, was installed c.1820. Before that villagers were served by a shallow well with a bucket and chain.

A parish school was established at Yarde in 1819 by Rector George Trevelyan. It took in 120 poor children, and those whose parents could afford it paid 2d. a week. A Sunday school was attended by 80 children at the same time, and this was still in existence at the time of the 1851 census, when it had 60 children on the roll. In 1835, Sir John Trevelyan, his son Walter, and the rector paid for the schooling of 42 children, and the rest, out of a total of 107, were paid for by their parents. In 1903 the premises were being leased to the rector and churchwardens by Sir Walter John Trevelyan at a peppercorn rent. The highlight of the year for the children was the visit by Lady Trevelyan at Christmas to present each child with a bag of sweets, and a pair of boots to the eldest child of each family.

In 1931, the senior pupils were transferred to Washford and Williton and only 29 children remained on the roll. Numbers fell still further during the next decade and in 1945, when there were only seven children on the books, the school was closed. The buildings were then shared between a private house and the Village Hall; the entire property subsequently became a private house.

The old school and Village Hall was the scene of many parish social events, including the presentation by the Nettlecombe Players of works by Phoebe Rees.

The Blade Mill by the main stream at Yarde was established in 1838 and worked by Edward Davis, later being used for storage purposes by Yarde Farm. It was renovated in 1990 and it is now a private dwelling. Yokes of oxen ploughed the fields locally in the 1850s, but were rarely seen after 1860; it is said that the ploughmen used to sing to them. In about 1890 severe flooding occurred at Yarde owing to heavy snowfall on the Brendons which quickly thawed due to excessive rain. This brought down debris which blocked the road arch near Yarde Farm, turning most of Yarde into a large lake. A fat pig belonging to Yarde Farm Cottage was swept over the wall of the roadway near the farm and was found drowned several days later at Stream, half a mile away. The depth of the water in the cottage was three feet and at the farm five feet.

Map of Yarde at the time of the Minehead Turnpike Trust's work there in 1822.

LOT 1 *(Coloured Pink on Plan No. 1 and Inset Plan No. 1)*

YARD FARM
Yard

159 a.   3 r.   38 p.
(159.990 Acres—See separate Schedule)

Description	Area	Tenant	Tenancy	Rent per annum
				£ s. d.
Yard Farm	158.245	Mr. W. J. Barnes ..	Yearly Michaelmas. Agreement dated 1st Oct., 1932	371 19 0*
Woodlands	1.745	In Hand	Vacant Possession	—
Shooting Rights ..	—	Mr. W. J. Barnes ..	Yearly, Verbal	10 0 0

* Apportioned

Outgoings: Tithe Redemption Annuity £39 8s. 3d. (informally apportioned).

AN EXCELLENT T.T. AND ATTESTED DAIRY FARM

situated on the north-east side of the Estate, about 3 miles to the south-west of Williton and about 8 miles from Minehead.

THE FARMHOUSE

is conveniently located on the south side of the public road in the centre of the holding.   It is mainly built of stone with a slated roof and has partly rendered elevations.   The accommodation comprises:—

On the Ground Floor: **Entrance Porch; Entrance Hall** with radiator; **Cloakroom** with basin (h. & c.) and low level W.C. suite; **Dining Room** with brick fireplace and two cupboards; **Drawing Room** with brick fireplace, china and store cupboards and radiator; **Kitchen** with store cupboard; **Scullery; Old Salting House** with sink, salting trough and two store cupboards; **Back Kitchen** with open fireplace, bread oven and copper, and **Fuel Store and Workshop** with cider press.   Below is a **Cellar.**

On the First Floor: Small Landing and Passage with trap door to roof space; **Five Bedrooms,** three with fireplaces and two with deep cupboards; and **Bathroom** with W.C. and range of cupboards.

Main Electricity.   Estate Water Supply.   Drainage to cesspool and stream.

Outside: Loft or Granary.   Kennel.   Ash Pit.

Garden with lawn and flower borders.

Sale particulars, 1957. Yarde Farm sold for £6,000.

THE FARM BUILDINGS

which are well situated near the Farmhouse, comprise:—Galvanised iron and asbestos-roofed **Cowhouse** for 12, with concrete standings, drainage channel, mangers, feeding passage and forecourt, tubular fittings and partitions and automatic water bowls; **Dairy** of breeze blocks, brick and asbestos roof with concrete floor; **Four-bay Dutch Barn** with covered way connecting to **Three-bay Dutch Barn,** both with steel stanchions and galvanised iron roofs and wind shields; **Wilmot Danish Piggery** with seven pens and store pen, central and feeding passages and feeding troughs built of galvanised iron by timber frame with concrete base and asbestos roof; **Two-bay Implement Shed; Three-bay Wagon House** of stone with thatched roof; **Cattle Yard or Court;** stone and galvanised iron **Calf House** divided into three pens, with mangers and hay racks; second **Cattle Yard or Court** with **Three-bay Open Shelter;** stone and slated range of **Three Calf Boxes** with mangers and hay racks and **Loft** over; stone and asbestos-roofed **Barn** with part concrete floor and Loft over one end; **Bull Pen** with concrete floor, feeding passage, manger and automatic water bowl; third **Cattle Yard or Court** with water trough and **Four-bay Open Cattle Shed** of stone and thatched roof, with manger and hay racks; **Loose Box** with manger, hay rack and automatic water bowl; lean-to stone and slated range of **Four Cattle Pens** with concrete mangers, hay racks and automatic water bowls; **Chicken Run** with two lean-to shelters; timber and asbestos **Two-bay Tractor Shed** with concrete floor; stone and slated **Stable Block** with concrete floor converted as **Garage, Two Corn Stores** and **Granary** over.

On the opposite side of the road is a stone and slated **Blade Mill** used for storage. In O.S. No. 272 is a stone and slated **Implement Shed.**

A MODERNISED DETACHED COTTAGE

is situated near the farm drive and conveniently close to the farm buildings. It is built of stone with a slated roof and contains:—**Entrance Porch; Living Room** with brick fireplace having back boiler for hot water supply, and cupboard; **Scullery** with sink (h. & c.); **Bathroom** with panelled bath (h. & c.) and low level W.C. suite; **Heated Linen Cupboard** with hot tank fitted with electric immersion heater; and **Two Bedrooms,** one with fireplace and cupboard with tank.

Main Electricity. Estate Water Supply. Cesspool Drainage.

Outside: Lean-to Coal and Wood Store. Garden Shed.
Large Flower and Kitchen Garden.

THE LAND

comprises four main parcels with a centrally-placed homestead and being intersected by public roads affording good access to most of the fields. Much of the land is fairly level but some portions slope south-westwards. Streams provide watering facilities to some enclosures. There is some hedgerow timber.

THE WOODLANDS

comprise Quarry Hill Copse of about 1 acre, which contains some well-grown oak, sycamore, sweet chestnut, larch and Scots Pine and a small copse, being O.S. No. 275, which contains mainly Scots Pine, larch and sycamore.

NOTES:
Rights of Way: This Lot is sold subject to a right of way for all purposes in favour of (1) Lot 2 between the points marked A—B and C—B on the Sale Plan No. 1, and (2) Lot 8 between the points marked D—E on the Sale Plan No. 1.
Yard Estate Water Supply: See Special Condition of Sale No. 7.

Above: *West Somerset Mineral Railway line maintenance men Billy Willis* (left) *and Jim Vickery on their trolley above Torre crossing, c.1908.*

Right: *Torre level crossing in 1938, showing the gatekeeper's hut, which still stands, with its 1871 datestone.*

The Auction Mart, close to Washford Railway Station, c.1900, where Mr William J. Leversha, of Torre, held livestock sales.

Torre

Tucked away at the far north-west of Nettlecombe parish is the almost hidden, peaceful hamlet of Torre. Around this part of the parish the farms and homesteads are linked by narrow lanes with high banks, the names of which derive from the farms or hamlets they serve. By the fourteenth century Torre had emerged as a hamlet, and grew during the eighteenth and nineteenth centuries when Nettlecombe village disappeared. Before 1838 roadside cottages were also built at Vempletts Cross, Egypt and Fair Cross.

There was more than usual activity in this part of the parish when the ceremony of cutting the first sod for the construction of the West Somerset Mineral Railway from Watchet to the Brendon Hills took place at Roughmoor, opposite Beggearn Huish, on 29 May 1856. Work then commenced on the section between Watchet and Roadwater. The first locomotive was brought from Taunton to Roadwater by November 1856, and a temporary shed was provided at Torre siding to house this engine. From Washford the line crossed the road to Fair Cross at Torre level crossing, which was the site of a siding used mainly for wagon repairs, a gatekeeper's hut (still standing) dated 1871, and a disc and crossbar signal. It was customary to pick up or set down passengers here, although it was not a station.

To the north of the old level crossing site is a disused quarry which, in its working days, supplied much of the stone for building the stations and bridges of the West Somerset Mineral Railway. The old quarry was later used as a rifle range by Old Cleeve branch of the British Legion.

At the end of the nineteenth century William J. Leversha established an auctioneer's business at Torre with offices in the large house on the left from the direction of the White Horse Inn, which is situated just over the parish boundary in the Washford ward of Old Cleeve parish. As can be seen from part of an advertisement which appeared in the *West Somerset Free Press* in October 1907, a train was scheduled to arrive at Washford Station from Taunton in time for the auction mart nearby. By 1910 William J. Leversha had amalgamated with John Risdon & Son, auctioneers, of Williton and Wiveliscombe, and the name of the new firm was Risdon & Leversha, auctioneers, of Wiveliscombe, Washford and Williton. During the 1920s the name Leversha disappeared from the firm, which was then known as Risdon, Gerard & Hosegood. Later, during the mid-1940s the firm's name was altered once again – this time to Risdon, Hosegood & Morle. After further name changes and take overs, it is gratifying that one of the old names still survives in the firm's title in 2003 – Hosegood Ford – who have offices at Williton and Porlock under the direction of the principal, David Hosegood.

Over the years many successful auctions, markets and Christmas fatstock shows were held at Washford on a site near the Railway Hotel (later named the Washford Hotel) until the market ceased in 1968, the site later becoming a housing estate.

Torre Farm was at one time farmed by James Stoate and, besides the farmhouse (now Torre House), had several farm workers' cottages associated with it. The site of the farm has been transformed with the conversion of the old barns and dairy into residences and a cider farm, where people can wander at leisure looking at a variety of animals, watch a video on cider-making and sample different varieties of cider straight from the barrels. Many old beams have been retained in the conversion.

Right: West Somerset Free Press *ad.*, 1907.

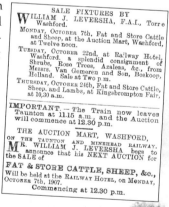

Cottages at Torre in the 1930s.

Above: *Enjoying a tasting at Torre Cider Farm on a fine summer's day in the 1990s. The building is a converted barn, in which one of the beams bears the date 1825 worked in nails.*

Above: *The old dairy at Torre Farm before conversion.*

Below: *The old dairy at Torre Farm after conversion in the mid-1980s.*

Below: *PC Terence Cheek holding the commendation certificate awarded to him by the Chief Constable of Somerset and Avon Police in 1989 for displaying great bravery in arresting a man armed with a shotgun. Terence spent many of his younger years at Torre with his parents, Mr and Mrs William Cheek.*

Aerial view of Torre, 1989.

Above and above right: *Torre House, formerly Torre Farmhouse; the porch (left) bears the date 1681 and the initials 'HB'.*

Right: *James Stoate of Torre, who farmed at Torre Farm for many years.*

Below: *The house at Torre from which William J. Leversha ran his auctioneer's business in the early 1900s.*

Above: *Nettlecombe Court and Parish Church, c.1900.*

Left: *Nettlecombe gardening staff, c.1905.*

Below: *Deer in Nettlecombe Park.*

Left: **The Trevelyan coat of arms above the front entrance to Nettlecombe Court.**

Nettlecombe Court

Nettlecombe's history can be traced back to Saxon times. Before the Norman Conquest it was held by Earl Godwin, son of King Harold, but after 1066 the manor reverted to the Crown. There were 50 acres of woodland at Nettlecombe in 1086, and during the nineteenth century timber from the Park was regularly sold for ship-building, church repairs and other purposes, some being shipped out from Watchet. There were no finer oaks than the old trees of Nettlecombe Deer Park (which today is used as an international seed bank), and when a tree in the Park was felled in 1931 it revealed a cannonball dating back to 1650.

During the reign of Henry II in the twelfth century, Nettlecombe was in the possession of John, son of Gilbert, Earl Marshal of England; he granted the manor to Hugh de Ralegh, of Ralegh in Devon, on the condition that he should find one soldier in times of war for two months and for 40 days in times of peace. In payment Hugh de Ralegh gave John 80 marks of silver and a sorrel nag; to his lady an ounce of gold; and to each of his sons a talent. The estate was confiscated during the reign of King John because the Ralegh of that day sided with the barons, but it was re-purchased by his brother, Warin de Ralegh.

Since then Nettlecombe Court has never been sold, passing by descent through the families of Ralegh, Whalesborough, Trevelyan and Wolseley. For nearly 300 years the Raleghs held Nettlecombe, one of the most famous of them being Sir Simon de Ralegh, a great warrior who spent five years fighting in France and was at the Battle of Agincourt. Towards the end of his years he retired to Nettlecombe where he founded and endowed a chantry to St John the Baptist on the south side of the Parish Church which sadly became a victim of the Reformation and was swept away in 1548.

By 1304 Rowdon manor in Stogumber parish was held with this manor and the two were generally administered as a single unit known as the manor of Nettlecombe and Rowdon.

According to a well-known Devon antiquary, Sir Walter Raleigh's family migrated from Nettlecombe; the founder of this branch of the family was Sir Wymondde Ralegh, who settled at Smallridge in the parish of Axminster. Sir Walter Raleigh himself made his home at Sherborne in Dorset.

Sir Simon de Ralegh, the warrior of Agincourt, was the last of the male line at Nettlecombe, and he left all his estates to his niece, who was the daughter of Thomas Whalesborough, of Whalesborough in Cornwall. This Thomas had only one child, Elizabeth, who was married in 1452 to Sir John Trevelyan, knight, of Trevelyan in Cornwall.

The Trevelyans were a very old Cornish family of yeoman stock, hailing from Lerryn and St Veep, near Fowey. The first at Nettlecombe was a man of much note in his time and was attached to the Lancastrian side in the Wars of the Roses. Most of his friends or associates died by sword or by axe during these wars, but he survived and succeeded, by means of a series of royal pardons, in holding his estates together; he died peacefully at Nettlecombe in 1489. Legend has it that the white horse rising from the water on the Trevelyan coat of arms, seen through the house at Nettlecombe, is supposed to represent the steed of the first member of the family which saved its master by swimming with him to the Cornish mainland after the mythical land of Lyonesse sank beneath the sea.

Demi-horse mounted on a gate pier at the entrance to Nettlecombe Court. A demi-horse rising from the sea forms part of the Trevelyan coat of arms.

Nettlecombe saw some stirring times when the Civil War broke out; the squire of that day, George Trevelyan, threw in his lot with King Charles and whilst away fighting for the King, the rector of Nettlecombe, fanatical Roundhead Robert Gay, led a party of rapscallions against the Court with every intention of burning it to the ground. He and his crew were not driven off until they had destroyed outbuildings up to the very door. Gay was imprisoned for his actions but later released and continued as rector until he died in 1671. When the Parliamentary forces won, George Trevelyan's estate was sequestrated or fined. A detachment of Parliamentary troops plundered his house and drove away cattle, sheep and horses. They failed, however, to find the family and church plate which had been transferred to the Court when the chantry chapel was suppressed at the time of the Reformation, for his wife Margaret had hidden it under the floor of one of the rooms. It is said that it was discovered there generations later when a maid sewing in the Tudor Room of the Court dropped her thimble, which rolled away and slipped through a crack in the floor. It was a precious thimble and a floorboard was taken up to look for it when, to everyone's astonishment, a quantity of Elizabethan and Jacobean plate and the Nettlecombe chalice and paten were revealed. The owner had reason for some of it to be sold, no doubt through force of circumstances as the estate had been robbed by war expenditure and the many fines paid to hold the estate together, but the chalice and paten were restored to the church.

Margaret Trevelyan had farm oxen yoked to the family coach and set out for London to plead on her husband George's behalf and obtain a pardon. After 12 months the House of Commons granted a full pardon, but imposed a further additional fine on her husband of £1,560, a tremendous sum for those times. It was December 1645 before Mrs Trevelyan

The Trevelyans and their staff, c.1926. Left to right, back row: J. Davis, T. Stevens, A. Burnett, S. Bennett, E. Stevens, J. Watts, J. Ford, W. Willis, W. Aplin; third row: B. Burge, W. Bryant, J. Maddock, J. Routley, H. Stevens, R. Smith, W. Stevens, H. Davis, E. Richards, P. Ford, J. Ford, H. Burnett; second row: E. Chilcott, Mrs A. Routley, Mrs Bryant, ?, ?, Mrs J. Willis, Mrs Allen, Miss Aplin, G. Hole, F. Willis, G. Routley, W. Somerfield, Mr Allen, H. Tarr; seated: Mr Tooze, J. Stone, J. Smith, Mr Le Fevre, Miss Urith Trevelyan, Lady Trevelyan, Sir Walter Trevelyan, Bt, Miss Joan Trevelyan, J. Bond, G. Routley, E. Hill, H. Ford, J. Ford; front: H. Routley, Maud Calloway, Vera Aplin, F. Willis.

Nettlecombe Harriers meeting at the Court, c.1900. The Harriers were established in 1895 by Sir Walter Trevelyan, who was an enthusiastic huntsman.

could leave London and head for home, but tragically she never arrived, dying of smallpox at Hounslow where she was buried, leaving her husband and 11 small children. George was finally discharged in 1649 after making a last payment of £230, but he did not live long to enjoy the possessions he had ransomed with such difficulty for he died aged only 39, and he was buried at Nettlecombe on 3 November 1653.

After the Restoration, George Trevelyan's sufferings for the Royal cause were rewarded when Charles II bestowed a baronetcy on his son George, who thus became the first Trevelyan baronet in 1661. The last baronet to live at Nettlecombe was Sir Walter John, 8th baronet, who died in 1931. He was a keen hunting enthusiast, who founded the Nettlecombe Harriers in 1895 and was also a steadfast supporter of the West Somerset Foxhounds. His only son, Willoughby John, succeeded to the title but lived away from Nettlecombe and the estate passed to Sir Walter's only surviving daughter, Joan Alys Trevelyan, later the wife of the artist Garnet Ruskin Wolseley, nephew of the famous Field Marshal Viscount Wolseley.

Sir Walter's younger daughter Urith died in 1929. It was through the initiative of Joan Trevelyan that the 1st Nettlecombe Company of Girl Guides was founded, and the good work she did in her capacity as its captain was reflected in her appointment as a district commissioner. Joan Wolseley died in 1943 and Garnet Wolseley in 1967.

The 9th baronet, Willoughby John, died – unmarried – in 1976; he was followed by a distant Californian cousin, whose son, Edward Norman Trevelyan, the 11th baronet, succeeded in 1996. The estate still belongs to the Wolseley family; the owner at the time of writing, John Walter Wolseley, an artist like his father, and his elder son, William Trevelyan Wolseley, live in Australia, but his younger son, Thomas Ralegh Wolseley, lives in England and does occasionally visit the estate.

Nettlecombe Court is a complex house of red sandstone with Ham-stone dressings. A hall, 11 chambers and five service rooms were mentioned in an inventory in 1525. The mansion house of today was largely rebuilt in 1690 by Sir John Trevelyan, but some of the former building, of late medieval date, was incorporated, as can be seen by items of pre-Tudor masonry in the present lower portions. The great hall, porch and oriel were built in 1599.

Miss Joan Trevelyan with Major Anstruther leaving Nettlecombe Court on her way to be married to Garnet Wolseley at Nettlecombe Church, 1937.

The old Deer Park at Nettlecombe, 2002.

Much landscaping was carried out at the estate by the second Sir John, and the idyllic setting was used to good effect in 1963 when it was the film location for 'Tom Jones', starring Vanessa Redgrave, Susannah York, Albert Finney, Hugh Griffiths and Wilfred Larson. Many local people took the opportunity to appear as 'extras'.

West Somerset Foxhounds meeting at Nettlecombe Court, c.1900.

Trevelyan Baronets Lineage

1. Sir George Trevelyan, at King Charles II's Restoration. Died 1671.
2. Sir John Trevelyan, a man of note who was MP for Minehead and High Sheriff for Somerset. Born 1670, died 1755.
3. Sir George Trevelyan, born 1707, died 1768. Married Julia, daughter and heir of Sir Walter Calverley and ultimate heir of Sir William Blackett, of Wallington in Northumberland.
4. Sir John Trevelyan, died 18 April 1828 at the age of 93. Married Louisa Marianne Simond.
5. Sir John Trevelyan, born 1 January 1761, died 1846. A kindly man who took good care of his tenants.
6. Sir Walter Calverley Trevelyan, a very studious man and great temperance advocate; was president of the United Temperance Alliance. He built the Temperance Hall at Roadwater and was the instigator of temperance meetings at Nettlecombe, at one time upwards of 1,200 persons being present in the Park, with welcome flags strung from tree to tree at Woodford. Born 1797, died 1879.
7. Alfred Wilson Trevelyan. He had five daughters and therefore no heir to the estates; died 1891, aged 60.
8. Sir Walter John Trevelyan, born 1866, died 1931. A greatly respected man. Married Alice Edith Money in 1901.

A Trevelyan family group. **Left to right:** *Louisa, Lady Louisa Marianne Trevelyan, Sir John Trevelyan, 4th Bt (1735–1828), a son (possibly John, later 5th Bt). By Arthur William Devis (original held by the National Trust, Wallington).*

The red stonework of the south front is of great merit, now exposed to view as the plaster and roughcast completed by Sir John Trevelyan, presumably to keep the building dry, was removed; this stonework was pointed by Sir Walter John Trevelyan. He also re-sited the demi-horses (the work of the second Sir John) on pillars at the Park entrance; they formerly stood on pillars leading to the kitchen court.

The second alteration was made c.1730–45, when the entrance hall was taken out of the great hall to form an organ gallery. The panelling of the great hall is of about the same date. The third phase was to build the west wing, this was done in 1787–88 with neo-classical decorations to enhance a magnificent suite of Adam furniture, which was sold at Christie's in 1957 for £7,500. The fourth phase, completed by Sir Walter Calverley Trevelyan, was the remodelling

of the kitchen and servants' quarters with additions. The fifth phase covered all new drainage and other sanitary arrangements, paving of the kitchen court, reinstating the second staircase and laying a new oak floor in the great hall, all of which was done by Sir Alfred Wilson Trevelyan.

North of the house is the stable block, which is dated 1792, and further north lay extensive kitchen gardens with a range of terraced greenhouses.

From the 1940s Nettlecombe Court was occupied by successive schools, the last being St Audries Junior School which remained until 1964. In 1967 the Court was leased by the Field Studies Council, converted, and is now known as the Leonard Wills Field Centre.

There were picturesque scenes in the grounds of Nettlecombe Court in August 1926. Just for a time

Left: *Miss Joan Trevelyan (with dog) and Williton and Nettlecombe Girl Guides at Nettlecombe Court, c.1920s.*

Second from bottom: *Estate workers outside the Village Hall at Yarde for Sidney Bennett's retirement, c.1950s. Left to right, back: Ernie Richards, Reg Ridler, Herbert Davis, Horace Routley, Bill Tregidgo, Arthur Burnett, Garnet Wolseley, Norman Fitton, Bill May, Jack Davis senr, Bill Willis, ?, Mr Booth, Harry Ford, George ('Porgie') Bryant, ?, ?, Jack Davis junr, ?, Harry Burnett; front: Sidney and Mrs Bennett, ?, ?, ?.*

Above: *Sidney Bennett, chauffeur to Lady Trevelyan, standing beside the Armstrong-Siddeley in Monte Carlo, c.1930s.*

A gathering at Nettlecombe Court during the late 1930s.

famous characters in English history came to life again and stirring events of the days of Good Queen Bess were enacted. Sir Francis Drake, who doubtless was a visitor at Nettlecombe when he came to court Elizabeth Sydenham of Combe Sydenham, appeared among the gallant company. Lord Howard of Effingham, admiral of the little English fleet which destroyed the hopes of Spain, re-enacted his famous role. Queen Elizabeth I was there in stately magnificence, and Philip II, the ambitious King of Spain, strutted awhile on the stage. A famous game of bowls was replayed, there was the clash of arms, the roar of cannon, the din of battle. All were elements in a pageant, 'The Armada 1588', which was presented in connection with the silver wedding celebration of Sir Walter J. Trevelyan, Bart., and Lady Trevelyan.

The farm workers in the employment of the tenantry of the Nettlecombe estate intended to make a presentation to Lady Trevelyan and Sir Walter on the occasion of the couple's silver wedding (16 July). With this in mind, Sir Walter not only invited them to a luncheon, but also organised a pageant for their entertainment. No subject perhaps for a pageant at Nettlecombe could have been more aptly chosen than that of the Spanish Armada since it introduced characters and incidents which by their association with the locality invested the performance with closer interest.

Sir Walter himself took part as King Philip; others who appeared in leading roles were Admiral Sir William Nicholson, KCB, DSO, and Capt. Nicholson, RN. Sir Walter spared no effort to give the pageant its proper historic atmosphere, and in its organisation Mr H.G. Tarr (sub-agent) and Mr H.E. Davis took a very active and helpful part.

First in order of the day's proceedings was the lunch given in the shade of immemorial trees adjoining the Deer Park, and here about 120 farm workers and others enjoyed Sir Walter's generous hospitality. Meanwhile, those taking part in the pageant, who included most of the estate employees and some of the household staff, were donning the colourful hired costumes of the period and getting ready for the performance. When the presentation took place, Queen Elizabeth I, seated in her royal chariot, with attendants and men-at-arms grouped about her, cut an impressive figure at the ceremony.

The presentation, to which about 80 farm workers had subscribed, consisted of two handsome silver vases, one of them bearing an inscription recording the circumstances of their presentation. The names of the subscribers to the presentation were recorded on a roll which accompanied the vases.

Mr G. Tarr, in making the presentation, said he wished the good feeling of the tenantry towards the owner was general throughout the country (it was the year of the General Strike), and added words of congratulation. Replying, Sir Walter gave a résumé of the Court's history and the distinguished families

associated with it, producing original documents from the unique collection in the muniment room.

The well-known story of the Spanish Armada was then enacted, while an alarm beacon blazed on Beacon Hill nearby, the actual spot of one of the chain of beacons lit at the time of the Armada. On the quarterdeck of *The Revenge* Lord Howard received the surrender and Queen Elizabeth I knighted the gallant English officer. Queen Elizabeth I gave thanks in St Paul's Cathedral, the invasion proclamation which was read being the actual contemporary document.

Queen Elizabeth I was played by H. Stevens; Lord Howard, Admiral Sir William Nicholson; Duke of Medina, Duke of Palma and Raleigh, Capt. Nicholson; Drake, A.J. Burnett; Seymour and the Cardinal, H.G. Tarr; Sir Christopher Hawkins, J. Hawkins; Sir William Frobisher, W. Bryant; King Philip II, Sir Walter Trevelyan; the Duke of Moncaldo, H.E. Davis. Other parts were played by Albert Ware, H. Napper, ? Knight (Chidgley), ? Webber (Chidgley), G. Routley, E. Calloway, A. Calloway, E. Allen, W. Hole, E. Richards, W. Somerfield, W. Willis, J. Watts, Joe Fold, D. Burge, J. Tooze, S. Watts, F. Willie, W. Bowden, F. Morse, Vera Aplin, Muriel Stevens, Horace Routley, Donald Tarr, Mr Bryant and P. Ford.

A social gathering of estate workers in the company of Garnet Wolseley and his son John, late 1940s.

Tea at the Court to celebrate the baptism of John Walter, son of Garnet and Joan Wolseley (centre), 1938. As well as family members, the tea was attended by guests, tenants and estate workers, and there were many presentations.

Queen's Coronation Celebrated

A comic football match between two scratch teams from the parish of Nettlecombe afforded considerable amusement as part of Queen Elizabeth II's Coronation Day celebrations on a showery 2 June 1953 at Yarde. This feature, one of many in a full day's entertainment, figured prominently in the evening programme. Arrangements for the day were made by a Coronation committee comprising the rector, the Revd G.M. Hickman (chairman), Messrs Garnet Wolseley, S. Bennett, W.J. Barnes and T. Somerfield, and Mesdames V. Notley, N. Fitton, E. Jones, R. Ridler and D. Davis, with the Misses J. Jones and M. Richards.

The proceedings opened in the Village Hall in the morning, when several parishioners witnessed the Coronation on television. In the afternoon tea was provided for all parishioners, being served by Mrs E. Jones (convenor) and lady helpers. The presentation of a crown piece to each child of the parish was sub-sequently carried out by Miss Jane Wolseley. Then all participated in a programme of sports arranged in a neighbouring field, where races were supervised by Mrs V. Notley and Mrs E. Trebble, with the assistance of the Misses J. Jones and M. Richards. At a social and dance in the Village Hall in the evening, Mr Barnes undertook the duties of MC. The proceedings concluded with a bonfire and fireworks.

Local Personalities

The late Tom Somerfield: Cecil Thomas Somerfield (always known as Tom) was born at Woodford in one of the original estate cottages built of stone taken from Nettlecombe's own quarry, and later lived only three doors away from his birthplace. He was the son of Walter (always known as 'Jesse') and Eva ('Bessie') Somerfield attended Yarde School. He became a house servant at Nettlecombe Court in 1937 at the age of 16, taking home just £2 per month. Tom's working relationship with the estate occupants was always a family affair; his father was employed by Lady Alice Trevelyan as Nettlecombe's head gardener, directing the running of the extensive walled gardens where apricots and peaches once ripened alongside the impressive greenhouses which were home to the vinery. Tom's sister, Beatie Taylor, also worked on the estate as a cook for the Wolseley family. When the Second World War broke out in 1939, Tom informed Lady Alice that he dreamt of being an air gunner in the Royal Air Force, but she valued him too highly to let him join up. She knew that as long as he was employed as an estate worker he would not be forced to enlist. Even a letter from the RAF to Lady Alice requesting her to release Tom for service was of no avail, so he had to remain at Nettlecombe. Tom always regretted not joining up; Lady Alice certainly had powers of persuasion! She departed for London in 1942, leaving the estate in the

hands of Mr and Mrs Garnet Wolseley, who continued to employ Tom.

In his father's day no less than 60 staff were employed to labour in the sta-bles, gardens and kitchens at the Court, but in 1948 Tom trod a new path, beginning, at the age of 27, a career as a stone mason, maintaining numerous farm buildings and stone walls belonging to the estate. Tom always carried the same stone hammer *(above)* to work which he had made in 1949 by a local blacksmith at Vellow at a cost of half a crown. The sandstone granary behind the Nettlecombe stableyard was Tom's first ever stone masonry job. He became highly skilled in his trade with a fine reputation, and it was Tom who carried out the stonework to set the bronze Madonna and Child into the wall at St Mary's Church, Nettlecombe, this being Mr Garnet Wolseley's memorial to his wife (formerly Joan Trevelyan).

Tom also built a 150ft stone rectory wall for neigh-bours at Woodford in the 1970s and charged them not a penny. He used to say that he worked as much for the sake of the company as for anything else. In later years Tom worked for just six months of the year, some of which were with a local builder and some directly for neighbours and friends who required repair jobs to be undertaken on their houses or garden walls.

A bachelor, Tom was of a very independent nature and would push a wheelbarrow to Williton and wheel two bags of coal back to Woodford, refusing any lifts. He was a prolific walker, especially after he broke a leg, and would walk to Taunton and back. In his younger days he played cricket for Nettlecombe and was a keen thespian with the Nettlecombe Players, appearing in many of Phoebe Rees' plays staged by the group. He was also a churchman and choir member.

Tom died in November 2000, aged 79, but his work throughout West Somerset remains as a testi-mony to him for all to see for many years to come.

Tom in his younger days and towards the end of his life.

The late Jim Waldock: James George Kenzie Waldock, better known as Jim, died in August 2002, aged 69, following a hospital operation. He was a popular and well-known local character, farming at Chidgley, where he regarded his farm and flock as a small corner of paradise, and was often to be seen riding around on his battered quad bike.

Jim was born in Surrey, but spent his childhood in the seaside village of St Agnes, on the North Cornish coast. There began his love for the countryside that was never to leave him. He was educated at Truro Cathedral School and, after working as a trawler-hand out of Newlyn, he joined the agricultural industry that was to become his life.

After serving an apprenticeship on a farm in Oxfordshire and then working at a homestead just north of Okehampton, Jim bought his first farm – Lilliput, near Bath – which he built up from a state of dereliction. Unfortunately, disaster struck when his dairy herd contracted foot and mouth, and it was said that, as far as dairy farming was concerned, he never fully recovered from the blow. In 1964, after a two-year stint at another farm near Bath, Jim and his family came to Chidgley.

Jim will be remembered as an affable, easy-going chap who was only too keen to stop for a cheerful chat. The esteem and affection in which he was held was reflected in the packed congregation which attended his funeral service at Nettlecombe Parish Church, when over 350 mourners were present.

The late Miss Phoebe Rees, OBE (d. aged 91 in January 1992): Phoebe Meirion Rees was born at Martock, the daughter of a parson, later vicar of Chipstable. Phoebe was christened after HMS *Phoebe* which, under the command of her great-grandfather, Captain Hillyer, defeated the American man-o'-war *Essex* in a battle in the War of 1812.

After attending school at St Anne's, Abbots Bromley, near Stafford, where she became head girl, she was accepted for a place at Newnham College, Cambridge, but in order to be near an aunt who was seriously ill she became a student at Birmingham University and graduated there. This change brought her into contact with the Birmingham Repertory Theatre, an experience which instilled in her a passion for drama.

After two years teaching English and history in London, Phoebe again responded to an appeal to look after her aunt, whose husband, the Revd Frederick Corfield, had become the rector of Nettlecombe, a position he held for 23 years. Thus began her association with West Somerset which was to last the rest of her life, firstly at the Rectory at Nettlecombe and then at her bungalow, The Sanctuary, at Five Bells, near Watchet. Whilst at Nettlecombe she became a close friend of the Trevelyan family. She also revived her love of drama and began writing plays, principally for village

dramatic societies and Women's Institutes. Her first play, *Thic Thare Dawg*, written in 1931 in Somerset dialect and based on an incident reported in the *West Somerset Free Press*, won such acclaim that it was subsequently broadcast in Bristol. It was the first of more than 50 plays, most of which were performed in village halls, barns, churches and small stages all over Somerset and the South West. A number were also performed in English-speaking countries abroad as well as in foreign languages, including Japanese – an achievement which earned Phoebe the OBE in 1974.

She also founded the Nettlecombe Players, who had a high reputation in county and regional drama festivals and, in 1939, won the Sybil Thorndike Trophy (a national award for the most enterprising drama team) for Phoebe's dramatisation of Thomas Hardy's *The Trumpet-Major*, in which she played the leading role. Her French Revolution play, *Intervention*, made £4,350 for charity when it was produced in London at The Strand Theatre just before the war.

Two of Phoebe's plays with themes of close local association have taken wing beyond the confines of Somerset. The first, *The White Dove of Bardon*, was originally written for radio, and after first being broadcast in the BBC West Region on Boxing Day 1948, was subsequently repeated on the Home Service and Overseas Service. The second, *The Miraculous Year*, concerns the time spent by Dorothy Wordsworth and her brother William at Alfoxden House, near Holford. It has been among the most successful and widely acclaimed of Phoebe's plays. Her achievement was all the more remarkable as she wrote the work after contracting the rare disease, sarcoidosis, in 1953, which eventually left her totally blind and, within six months, had turned her auburn hair silver. For a time she also became deaf, and recalled with joy the moment of recovery when suddenly she could hear the birds again. Phoebe taught herself touch-typing and, supplemented by dictation onto audio tapes, she completed not only the manuscript for *The Miraculous Year*, but

Phoebe on her 90th birthday.

Fred Corfield with Phoebe and great-nieces Cherry (left) and Sorrell Corfield.

went on to write further scripts. Another of her works, *Marriages Are Made in Heaven*, has a very local flavour and is based on the romance between Francis Drake and Elizabeth Sydenham.

The Nettlecombe Players in **Thic Thare Dawg**, *the first of many plays written by Phoebe Rees. The play came second in the Village Drama Festival of 1931 and was broadcast the same year.* **Left to right:** *Eva ('Bessie') Somerfield, Revd F.B. Corfield, Frances Watts, Nancy Routley, William Hole; seated on the box with Nell the dog is Phoebe Rees.*

Above: *Phoebe in costume for one of her many plays, c.1930s.*

Above: *The Nettlecombe Players in Davey Jones' Locker, 1933.* Left to right, back row: *Frank Stevens, Revd Fred Corfield, ?, Mrs Bryant, Miss Corfield, Nancy Routley, Phoebe Rees, Eva ('Bessie') Somerfield;* sitting: *Agnes Potter, William Hole, Tom Somerfield, Barbara Lamming, ?.*

Left: *The cast of* The Trumpet-Major *performed by the Nettlecombe Players, 1939.*

Right: *Programme for* The Trumpet-Major.

Below: *Tom Somerfield in costume for his part in* The Trumpet-Major.

Top: *Nettlecombe Players performing* Saint Cecilia's Slipper *outside Yarde School Hall, 1932.* Left to right: *Nancy Routley, Barbara Lamming, Mrs Wade, Mrs Bryant, Miss Corfield, Mary Pepperell (on pedestal), Phoebe Rees, Verna Davis, Muriel Stephens, Agnes Potter, Muriel Wade, Eva ('Bessie') Somerfield.*

Right: *The Sybil Thorndike Trophy won by the Nettlecombe Players in a national amateur-dramatics competition in 1939.*

❧ Extracts from Nettlecombe/Yarde School Log-books, 1897–1945 ❧

The following extracts make fascinating reading and reflect wider social changes. No names have been mentioned here where embarrassment might be caused, and only initials have been inserted in certain places. The school was closed in March 1945, the seven children being transferred to Monksilver School. The log-books are kept at the Somerset Record Office at Taunton.

1897

5 July   Attendance not good – whortleberry gathering the cause.

2 August Very small school, children still picking whortleberries – weather very hot.

4 Oct.   Standard II very backward in arithmetic.

22 Oct.   Winifred, Willie and Stanley Hosegood at home through illness. Average attendance 31.

18 Nov.   Mr F. Hosegood visited and looked at the writing and arithmetic.

Dec.   During the Christmas holidays, through the liberality of Sir Walter J. and Lady Trevelyan, one child of each family attending the school has had, as usual, a pair of boots. Lady and Miss Trevelyan came to the school and presented the boots, also giving each child a Christmas card.

1898

22 Feb.   No school today, children unable to come on account of the severe weather – snow on the ground.

22 March Admitted Ellen Bulpin from Stream (infant).

28 March Admitted Alice Chorley from Stream.

15 June   School small today, most of the Stream children gone to the seaside.

14 July   Very small school – whortleberry picking commenced.

1899

7 Feb.   Standard V did their composition very carelessly today.

14 Sept.   Have examined the registers and find them correct – Frederick Hosegood (manager).

1900

5 Jan.   Miss Trevelyan and several visitors from Nettlecombe Court visited the school; Miss Trevelyan gave the children boots.

10 April   Miss Trevelyan visited and looked at the girls' needlework.

8 Oct.   Several children away picking acorns.

17 Dec.   Infants much improved in reading.

1901

3 May   Admitted new scholar, Eva Bosley (infant).

10 Oct.   All the children from Stream gone to a tea-treat.

25 Nov.   Standard I very backward in arithmetic.

1902

25 April   Average attendance 28.

1903

5 Jan.   Small attendance – Maud Davis absent through illness.

20 Feb.   The [eldest] child of each family attending the school received a pair of boots, the gift of Sir Walter and Lady Trevelyan.

30 Sept.   This morning I, Vella Holder, commenced work in this school as mistress. I find that there are no exercise books in the school.

6 Nov.   The attendance was not so good this afternoon as some children went down to Williton for the carnival.

1904

12 April   Admitted a new scholar (infant), Ada Chorley, aged three years, and in the afternoon I admitted another scholar (infant), Daisy Short, aged four years.

13 April   Edith, John and Ellen Takle are suffering from whooping cough and have been forbidden to attend school by Dr Killick, of Williton.

29 April   Whooping cough has increased so much that Dr Killick has recommended that the school be closed until 6 June.

9 Sept.   George and Horace Notley have left to attend Queen's College, Taunton.

1905

25 May   R.R. and H.K. were being troublesome that afternoon and, after warning them, they had two stripes given them on the left hand.

19 July   Several children were away today at the Wesleyan Sunday School treat in connection with the Williton Wesleyan Chapel.

1 August There was no school this afternoon, it being the children's annual school treat at Blue Anchor.

6 Oct.   The children who stay in for dinner were swinging on the beam in the verandah, and on being told to take down the rope, pretended to obey. A quarter of an hour afterwards they were doing it again, so were all punished.

1906

9 Jan.   School re-opened – 24 children present, 27 on the registers.

12 Feb.   Kate Hunt scalded her feet on Saturday last and will not be able to attend school for a time.

16 March Cyril Hosegood is absent with a bad throat.

24 April   School re-opened with attendance of 22, Cyril Hosegood being absent through sickness. Stanley Hosegood has left to attend Queen's College, Taunton.

27 July   Annual school treat to St Audries.

1907

21 Feb.   Mr F. Hosegood visited the school this afternoon and checked the registers, which were found to be correct.

6 June   Lady Trevelyan visited the school this afternoon and, after hearing III and IV read, inspected the girls' sewing.

8 Aug.   School closed today for the summer holidays. The annual school treat will be at Blue Anchor tomorrow.

9 Sept.   School re-opened this morning with an attendance of 27, three boys being absent.

20 Dec.   Lady Trevelyan presented the usual Christmas gifts of boots and sweets to the children.

1908

13 March Lucy Webber is still absent with a bad throat.

1 July   Reported a boy for swearing.

7 Sept.   Admitted Hilda Pearce, aged 5.

23 Nov.   F.P. is under treatment for enlarged tonsils at the Taunton Hospital.

27 Nov.   Mr F. Hosegood visited the school and inspected the children's work.

18 Dec.   The attendance has been a record one this week, no child being absent, first time for several years 100%.

1909

13 Jan.   Alfred Tipper, of Stream, is absent and is said to be suffering from mumps.

3 March   Snow on the ground, poor attendance.

28 April   Five children absent this afternoon; they have probably gone to Fossett's circus at Williton!

24 June   Mr F. Hosegood visited the school and signed the registers.

20 July   Florence Chorley, Edwin Pugsley, Charles Ford and Dorothy Bryant are absent picking 'worts'.

6 Aug.   The school treat took place at Blue Anchor, where the children were conveyed in wagons kindly lent by Mr F. Hosegood and Sir Walter Trevelyan.

7 Sept.   School was re-opened with an attendance of 22. Cyril Hosegood has left and Herbert Joseph Pearse (infant) admitted.

18 Sept.   Francis Pugsley was kicked in the forehead by a horse yesterday.

13 Dec.   Francis Pugsley returned this morning after two months' absence.

23 Dec.   Lady Trevelyan presented the usual Christmas gifts, and Master Willoughby Trevelyan and Miss Joan Trevelyan recited Mr Nobody and My Dolly. The children sang carols.

1910

1 Feb.   On being questioned as to the reason of their absence, the boys of a family said it was because their mother had no food for them until tea-time.

7 April   Mrs M. Hobbs took charge of the

Nettlecombe/Yarde School, c.1912, with Miss A.A. Babb (head teacher) on the far left and Miss Enid Evered (teacher).

school as temporary teacher. Admitted Jamie, Thomas and Fred Takle from Torre.

22 April   Only seven children turned up this afternoon, the others having gone to a circus at Williton.

2 May   Miss A.A. Babb entered upon her duties as head-teacher.

9 May   Admitted John Routley.

23 May   Admitted Flora and Leslie Headford – now 26 children on books.

24 June   Revd C.S. Dupuis visited the school.

3 Oct.   The monitress, Mary Bosley, has left and Annie Ford appointed in her place.

1911

23 Feb.   Only eight children present this morning owing to a great epidemic of measles. Received orders from Dr Savage to close school until 20 March.

27 March   Twenty-three children present out of 26.

6 July   Mr F. Hosegood visited the school and tested the registers.

25 July   Fifteen children were absent this afternoon, attending the Washford Wesleyan Sunday School treat at Minehead; 19 children present.

1912

20 Dec.   Lady Trevelyan visited the school and gave her usual gifts of sweets and boots to the children, she also gave a nice book to Percy and Joseph Ford for having made perfect attendance during the year.

1913

6 Jan.   Re-opened the school with 32 children present.

7 Feb.   Enid Evered resumed her duties as monitress today after being absent for five weeks owing to an outbreak of measles at her home.

1914

5 Jan.   Re-opened school with 30 children present. Admitted John Chick, aged five.

14 March Flora Headford sat for the Labour Certificate examination at Minehead and passed; she has now left school. Ada Chorley has also left. There are 29 on books.

7 Sept.   School re-opened, 22 children present out of 35. Admitted Stanley, Thomas and Bessie James.

23 Dec.   Lady Trevelyan, Miss Joan, Miss Urith and Master Willoughby visited the school and presented the usual Christmas gifts. Joseph Ford has again made perfect attendance for the year.

1915

29 July   School closed this afternoon on account of the annual school treat at Blue Anchor.

1916

10 Jan.   Re-opened school with 34 children present, 38 on books. Admitted Donald Barnes.

1 March Very bad weather, deep snow on ground – only 20 children.

1917

23 April   Admitted Ivy Chick; there are now 36 children on books.

1918

22 Oct.   Miss Robinson visited the school this afternoon and examined the needlework. She again awarded us the mark 'Excellent',

this being the fifth year in succession we have gained this distinction.

12 Nov.   A holiday given today in honour of the signing of the Armistice.

11 Dec.   Obliged to close the school owing to an epidemic of influenza – did not open again until after the Christmas holidays.

1919

30 May   Only 19 children present the whole of this week, 13 being absent suffering from influenza. School to close for while.

17 June   Mr Leng, the County Committee's Inspector, visited the school today. Report: 'This is an excellent village school in a remote country parish where teachers and managers are interested in the work. The tone and discipline are very good and the children are under very good influence...'.

1920

15 Jan.   Nurse Mills visited the school this afternoon and was much pleased with the clean appearance of the children.

22 Jan.   No school today – Sir Walter and Lady Trevelyan gave the children a great treat, sent them by train to Taunton to see the pantomime, Mother Goose.

24 Dec.   The Misses Trevelyan visited the school this morning and distributed the usual gifts of boots and sweets to the children. Eleven children made perfect attendance during the year, and each child received a book from Lady Trevelyan.

1921

5 Sept.   The supplementary teacher, Miss Enid Evered, has now left after 10 years' good work and Mrs Davis has been appointed in

Left: *The school, c.1920. Left to right, back row: Miss Enid Evered, ? Gould, Jenny Headford, Grace Gould, Mary Pepperell, Gertie Hill, ?, ?, Miss Babb; amongst others: Violet, Margaret and Charlie Headford.*

Below: *Yarde School opened in 1819, closed in 1945 and was then the Village Hall, but is now a house.*

Right: *Nettlecombe/Yarde School, 1928. Left to right, back row: Mrs Davis, D. Chamberlain, B. Yeandle, M. Chamberlain, I. Hayes, B. Somerfield, ?, D. Sampson, Miss Babb; middle rows include: V. Dunn, P. Chamberlain, G. Comer, M. Towells, T. Somerfield, M., J. and H. Fouracre, M. Wade, D. Hayes; front: F. Stevens, V. Chamberlain, ?, S. Chamberlain, ?, H. Davis, H. Sampson, C. Headford.*

her place; she commenced work this morning.

11 Nov. The Revd C.C. Sharpe visited the school this morning and gave the children an address on 'Armistice Day'.

1922

13 Feb. Muriel Stevens and Beatrice Somerfield are absent through sickness.

28 Feb. A whole day's holiday was given in honour of Princess Mary's wedding.

3 March Wretched attendance this week – nine children absent with influenza.

10 March Mrs Davis has been absent three days this week, being in bed with a very bad influenza cold.

1923

16 May Closed the school for three weeks owing to an outbreak of measles.

25 July No school this afternoon on account of the annual school treat to St Audries.

8 Oct. On Saturday morning we received news of the death of Phyllis Routley.

1924

7 Feb. Sixteen children visited the dentist this morning at Mrs Pepperell's cottage.

6 May Winnie Churcher absent from school, measles.

2 Sept. Muriel Stevens has now left to attend Bishop Fox's, Taunton.

1925

6 Jan. There are now 30 on the books. Mr Garle very kindly gave the children a tea and

magic lantern entertainment.

29 June Holiday today in order that the children should go to their annual school treat, this year to Burnham.

21 Sept. Admitted Florence, Lillian, Beatrice and Ethel Fifuel from Leighland.

1926

28 April Commenced school at 1 pm sharp to enable children to go to a circus at Williton.

1927

2 March Received notice from Dr Savage to close the school until Monday, 7 March, on account of so many children being away with influenza and severe colds.

7 March Opened school, 26 present. The Chamberlain family still away, very poorly.

22 June No school this afternoon on account of a fete being held in Nettlecombe Park.

1928

17 April The dentist visited Mrs Pepperell's house – 22 children were presented for treatment.

17 May A holiday was given today to enable children to journey to Swindon to go over the works of the GWR.

24 May Today being Empire Day, the Rector visited the school.

11 June Nurse Mills visited the school this morning and sent home three children with dirty heads.

9 Oct. Commenced school at 1 pm to

enable mistress and choirboys to attend the funeral of the Rt Hon Sir Arthur Channell.

1929

26 July Received notice that Muriel Wade and Frank Stevens had won 'free places' to attend Minehead Secondary School.

9 Dec. Owing to the very rough storms and flooded state of the roads, only 18 children were present.

1930

14 March Harold Davis, Hubert Bragg and Lillian Bryant sat for the 'free place' examination today. Revd F.B. Corfield, Mrs Wonnacott and Miss Corfield acted as invigilators.

26 May Received notice that Harold Davis, Hubert Bragg and Lillian Bryant had passed part I of the 'free place' examination.

27 Oct. John, Hubert and Mary Fouracre have now, with the doctor's sanction, returned to school after three months' absence; Donald Hayes also returned after eight weeks' absence.

1931

7 Jan. Re-opened school with 35 children present. Admitted Cyril and Jean Burnett.

25 May Received notice that Frances Watts passed Part I of the 'free place' examination.

27 May Received notice from the Education Committee that all children of 11 years of age and over were to proceed to Williton and Washford schools on Monday,

1 June – this school therefore becoming a junior school from that date.

1 June Re-opened school; admitted Barbara Bryant (infant). There are now 15 in the upper division and 14 in the lower.

31 July I this day resign the post of head-teacher of Nettlecombe/Yarde School – A.A. Babb.

1932

11 Jan. Commenced duty as headmistress – Ellen Lamming.

22 June Mr White (headmaster of Williton School) visited this afternoon for a conference.

1933

24 May Empire Day – patriotic celebrations.

20 Dec. Lady Trevelyan visited the school and made usual presentations of prizes, boots and sweets.

1934

2 March Examined registers – Phoebe M. Rees.

2 May School journey to Taunton, children paying own fares.

1935

6/7 May School closed for Royal Jubilee. Tea and sports for all parishioners; mugs and plates for all children at Nettlecombe Court.

6 Nov. School closed for wedding of Duke of Gloucester and Lady Alice Scott.

1936

20 Jan. Death of His Majesty King George V.

22 Jan. Listened to the Proclamation of King Edward VIII, broadcast from St. James's Palace.

1937

14 April School closed for the marriage of Miss Joan Trevelyan.

15 April Took children to Nettlecombe Court to see the wedding presents – at the invitation of Lady Trevelyan.

11 May Closed for Coronation (12 May) and Whitsun.

5 July School re-opened after being closed for six weeks through whooping cough. Jean Burnett has obtained a 'free place' at Minehead County School.

31 Aug. Re-opened after holiday, all 15 children present. Mrs Davis has left and is teaching at Monksilver School.

1938

24 June M. Richards and N. Knight have gained 'free places' at Minehead County School.

1939

23 June School journey to Weston-super-Mare.

29 Aug. School re-opened, seven out of eight present.

31 August School closed for national emergency.

11 Sept. School re-opened.

1940

8 Jan. School re-opened, all seven children present.

14 May Special instruction – national emergency.

1941

7 March 'Free places' examination – G. Webber, P. Barnes and B. Jones successful.

23 May Received 20 children evacuees from Bristol – Mr Thomas in charge.

16 June Received nine more senior boys from Monksilver.

2 Sept. Re-opened – senior boys now at Williton.

1942

11 June Mr Barnes mowed the playground with the tractor.

21 June Hay carried away.

8 Dec. Diphtheria inoculation.

1943

21 Jan. Closed for measles.

8 Feb. Re-opened – six present.

22 May Joyce Jones passed 'free place' examination.

1944

10 Jan. Re-opened, 10 out of 13 children present.

17 May Cherry Corfield passed 'free place' examination.

1945

25–31 Jan. School closed – deep snow.

Nettlecombe/Yarde School, c.1930s. Left to right, back row: Lillian Bryant, ?, Sid Chamberlain, Victor Chamberlain, Frank Stevens, ?, ?; third row: ?, ?, Charlie Headford, ?, ?, Bill Chamberlain, Bill Hayes, ?, ?, Harold Davis; second row: Gladys Coomber, Betty Yeandle, Ida Hayes, Marjorie Chamberlain, Miss Babb, Mrs Davis, Edna Davis, ?, Dorothy Chamberlain, Dorothy Sampson; front: Herbert and John Fouracre, ?, Winnie Lang, ?, ?, Valerie Dunn, Frances Watts, ?, ?, ?.

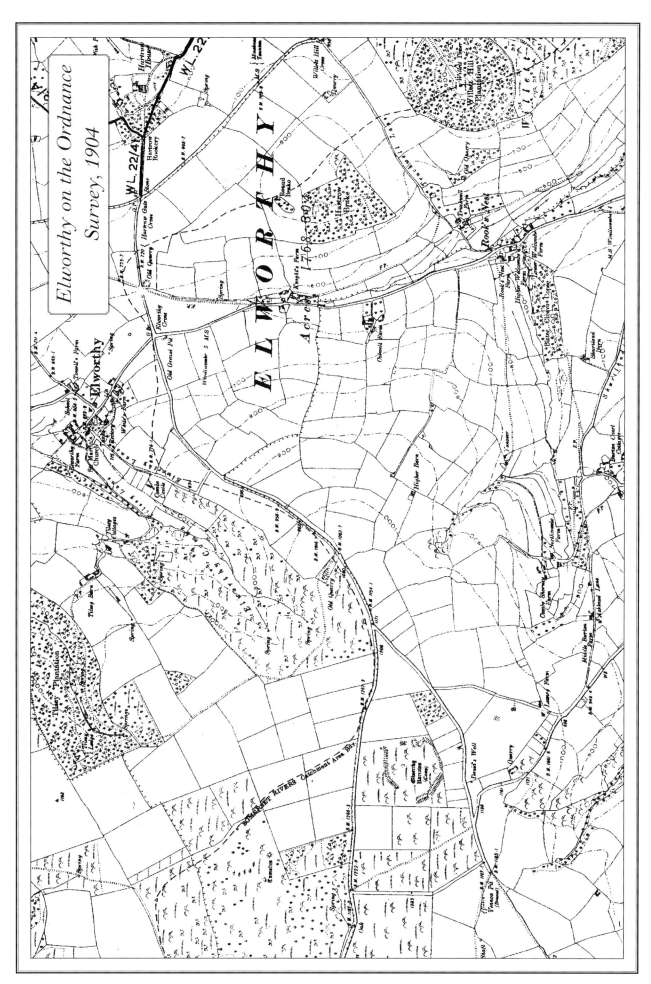

Elworthy on the Ordnance Survey, 1904

Four

Elworthy

The small parish of Elworthy was probably once part of the minster estate of Stogumber. It lies on the eastern slopes of the Brendon Hills, much of it falling within the Exmoor National Park. Elworthy village, with its revitalised buildings and delightfully-named Sun and Moon Cottage, is two miles south of Monksilver and a quarter of a mile north of the crossing of the Watchet–Wiveliscombe road and the Bampton-Taunton road, which were both turnpiked in 1806. The toll-house was at Elworthy Cross House, and there were gates on each road except that leading to the village. A route between Brompton Ralph and Stogumber which ran east of Elworthy village, avoiding the toll-house, was called Save Penny Lane but only lasted until 1827.

In 1667 there were 244 people listed in the parish, but the population fell sharply from 162 to 110 between 1891 and 1901. In 1981 there were only 78 people in Elworthy but in 2001 this had risen to 100.

Elworthy means 'Ella's clearing', after a Saxon named Ella, who felled woodland and planted a settlement on this site. Centuries before an Iron-Age population left an uncompleted fortress 1,200 feet above sea level and one mile south-west of the village – this is known as Elworthy Barrows. It was planned as a refuge place for people with cattle at a time of invasion and a prehistoric trackway runs nearby, which was later used by pack trains of wool merchants travelling across the Brendons.

The Parish Church of St Martin of Tours dates from the thirteenth century and it first occurs in written records in 1233 when William Malet gave it to the Order of St John of Jerusalem. St Martin was Bishop of Tours, France, in the fourth century. The western tower and two tiny lancet windows survive from the thirteenth century.

An Elworthy man named Henry Sweeting appeared before the archdeacon in 1623 'For making hay upon the Saboth day after evening prayer' and was ordered to 'admit his offence before the minister, wardens and eight others after evening prayer.' During the seventeenth century one of the most distinguished local families was that by the name of Lacey of nearby Hartrow Manor, in Stogumber parish. In the 1600s the chancel was so full of private

pews for the Laceys and their like that the church-wardens complained that the other parishioners had no room to 'draw near' to receive Holy Communion. The present nineteenth century screen commemorates the family and includes their coat of arms and crest.

The church is quite small, consisting of a tower, nave, chancel, northern porch and the southern extension of 1846. The walls are built of local material and the roofs covered with Treborough slates. Although of thirteenth-century origin, the tower received its present squared belfry windows and battlements in the 1700s. In the tower there is an interesting ring of four bells, which were rehung in a new oak frame in 1921 by Stogumber craftsman John Sully. Repairs to the tower were carried out in the late-twentieth century. The communion table and rails, which were installed c.1695, still survive, and from the same century is the striking font carved out of alabaster, probably from Watchet. In the churchyard stands a huge yew tree, reputed to be amongst the oldest in England. It is said that while conducting a committal service under the tree in 1708 the minister, Alexander Morley, dropped down dead.

The Rectory house was rebuilt about 1838 and the church was very considerably restored in 1846. The patronage was transferred in 1919 as a free gift by Mrs Somerset Gardner-McTaggart, probably mother of the incoming rector of Monksilver with Elworthy, to the dean and canons of Windsor, patrons of Monksilver, pending the union of the two parishes. The last resident rector left in 1919, his successor living in Monksilver. The old Rectory is now a private house.

In 1969 the living became a chapelry within the parish of Monksilver, as part of the united benefice of Monksilver with Brompton Ralph, Nettlecombe and, from 1977, Stogumber. The church was declared redundant in 1979 and vested in the Redundant Churches Fund. However, it still remains as part of the Quantock Towers Benefice.

The tower on Willett Hill had been built, 'at the expense of neighbouring gentry', by 1782, in the form of a ruined church and tower. Willett House, in its majestic setting, was built c.1816 by Richard Carver

🌿 The Church of St Martin 🌿

Far left: *Mr and Mrs Bill Stephens sitting in the armchairs which were presented to them in appreciation of 25 years of dedication and care to Elworthy Church and churchyard. The present was given as part of Elworthy's celebrations of King George V's Silver Jubilee in 1935.*

Above: *This was also presented in 1935 to Mr and Mrs Stephens as a mark of esteem for their 25 years of faithful service as sexton and caretaker respectively in the Church of St Martin, by the members of the congregation named at the foot of the citation.*

Right: *The enormous yew tree in Elworthy churchyard, one of the oldest such trees in England. Its girth is almost 30 feet, indicating an age approaching 850–1,000 years.*

The former Rectory at Elworthy, 2003.

The Church of St Martin of Tours, Elworthy.

Celebrating King George V's Silver Jubilee at Elworthy, 1935.

for Daniel Blommart, and by 1840 the parkland around the house had been created, being extended later that century. The house is a square structure with a main south front of five bays and two storeys. There is also a lower service wing, a courtyard, stables and coach-house. Among previous owners were the Cadbury family of chocolate fame. A later owner was Mrs Susanne Beadle, whose husband Fred was one of the founders of the British Field Sports Society (now part of the Countryside Alliance). The owner of Willett House at the time of writing is Mrs Rosemary Cox, MBE, whose well-deserved award in the Queen's Birthday Honours of 2003 was in recognition of her work and support for Macmillan Cancer Relief in Somerset. She is a former chairman of Somerset's Macmillan Trust, and was responsible for co-ordinating the county's ten fund-raising committees and its hundreds of volunteers. Over the years she has hosted many fund-raising events at her home, Her Majesty's Band of the Royal Marines even performing a concert there. Mrs Cox has helped to raise over £2 million for cancer since 1990.

Stock raising in the parish was principally centred around sheep, and a farmer's livestock tended to be worth twice as much as his crops in the seventeenth century. Out of 36 families in 1840, 30 were engaged in agriculture and only four in handicrafts. The farms tended to be few and sizeable, the largest being Plash and Willett with 307 acres, Elworthy Farm had 202 acres and Higher Willett, Lower Willett and Coleford Farms were each over 100 acres. The lord of the manor, Daniel Blommart, owned 1,215 acres out of a total of 1,635. During the 1970s there were at least 700 acres of grass supporting 846 sheep and 510

cattle. Plash Farm is of seventeenth-century origin or earlier and Elworthy Farm of the seventeenth or early-eighteenth century. Willett Farm was built in 1874, replacing the former fifteenth-century Willett farmhouse.

In 1826 20 children were attending school daily, and a free Sunday school was started in 1831. A school building was erected at Elworthy village in 1839 in union with the National Society, and this was supported by voluntary subscription. By 1847 16 boys and 14 girls attended the day school and 20 boys and 16 girls the Sunday school. Between 1875 and 1883 the school appears to have closed, but another was opened in a cottage at Willett for 40 children. A National school was opened at Elworthy in the old schoolhouse in 1892 for 30 children, but 42 were enrolled. During the next 40 years, however, numbers fell sharply, with only 12 children attending the school by 1933. It was closed in 1937, the children at that point transferring to Monksilver and Williton. The building was used for church purposes until 1951, the site later being conveyed for a village hall. This closed around 1965 and is now a private house.

The watch at Elworthy in 1556 was connected with firing beacons and other defences. The presentment to the Court Baron of Elworthy and Willett of 1682 is the only known record of a Manor Court. By 1829 there was a poorhouse in Cott Lane, in Elworthy Combe, west of the village, and this was ordered to be sold in 1858, when it comprised four cottages. It is thought to have been demolished in the late 1850s. From 1836 the parish was part of Williton Poor Law Union and of Williton Rural District from 1894. It has formed part of West Somerset District since 1974.

❧ Farming ❧

Above: *Rabbits caught at harvest time on Mr Tom Grandfield's farm at Elworthy, early 1930s. Left to right: Mr Powell, T. Grandfield, Bill Stephens junr, Bill Stephens senr, Robert Stephens.*

Left: *Elworthy Farm after a heavy frost, 2003.*

Harvesting at Elworthy Farm, c.1930. **Left to right:** *Mrs R. Stephens, Bill Stephens, ?, Bill Stephens junr (leading horse).*

❧ Willett ❧

Above: *Marjorie Sully and Hedley Hann at the water spout at Willett, 1935.*

Right: Mrs *Rosemary Cox, MBE.*

Left: *View of Willett Tower from Elworthy Barrows, 2002.*

Below: *Willett, 2002.*

Hunt meet at Willett House, c.1950.

Some of the Stephens family of Elworthy, c.1930.
Left to right: ?, Mrs Rose Stephens, Robert, Albert, Jack and William.

Right: *Formerly the school at Elworthy, now a private residence.*

Below: *Justin Williams and Jane Cleal with one of their hand-crafted pieces of furniture. E9stablished in 1990, they operate from Willett Farm Workshops and specialise in commissions for high-class furniture and individually made fitted kitchens.*

Right: **Well-known Elworthy farmer Edgar Thomas holding a pair of week-old lambs, 2003. Edgar is also a keen motorcycle enthusiast.**

This image: *The standing stone marking the highest point on Elworthy Barrows.*

❦ *Extracts from Elworthy CE School Log-books, 1892–1937* ❦

The following extracts make fascinating reading and reflect wider social changes. No names have been mentioned here where embarrassment might be caused, and only initials have been inserted in certain places. The log-books are kept at the Somerset Record Office at Taunton. On 30 July 1937 Elworthy Church of England School closed and the children transferred to Monksilver and Williton Schools. Miss Webb, head teacher of Monksilver School, and Mr W.J. White, head of Williton School, both went to Elworthy School for the purpose of dealing with the stock and apparatus.

1892

1 March This school was opened by me at 9 am today – 22 children entered in the morning, six more in the afternoon – Mary Anne Tyzack.

4 March Work very elementary. Classes formed according to ability, several children of seven and eight years do not know their letters and others 11 to 13 only fit for Standard I.

11 March Now 35 on books. Severe snow-storm on Wednesday prevented a number of children attending.

30 March Elizabeth, Tom, Bessie, Jane, Kate and Minnie Thorn leaving parish (Lady Day changes).

12 May Average attendance 22.9.

24 June William Lee having scarlet fever, the whole family (four children) were sent home for two months by order of Dr Brettingham. Very wet and only 11 children attended.

18 July Admitted infant Edith Mary House.

5 Sept. Resumed school, 19 in attendance. The Welshes and Yeandles away with whooping cough.

2 Dec. Average attendance for week 25. Little Ellen Horsey died last Tuesday after three weeks' illness.

1893

13 Jan. Severe cold. Children worked fairly well.

24 March School closed on Wednesday afternoon – the annual meet of Taunton Harriers at Willett.

7 April Work fair. Boys kept away, half day's potato planting.

May Inspector's Report (part): 'The children of this little school are well behaved and are being carefully and successfully taught. The porch where the hats and coats are hung requires a door. The entrance to the boys' closets is very near the road and the earth wall is not high enough.'

7 July On Thursday the Revd Morice brought a flag to hang on the porch and gave the children a half-day holiday for the occasion of the Royal Wedding.

14 July On Wednesday afternoon the children were taken to the Rectory where the Revd and Mrs Morice entertained them, their parents and friends to a tea and evening's amusements.

1 September School re-opened – Emily and Cecilia Welsh admitted on

Thursday. The same day an invitation from Mrs Blackwood, of Willett House, asking the school mistress to take the children to tea on Saturday. Fred Singleton left school to work at Hartrow Manor as odd boy. He has passed Standard IV and is nearly 13 years.

21 Dec. On Tuesday only one boy was brave enough to turn out due to severe weather. On Thursday children were treated to a 'snapdragon' and were also given Christmas cards and sweets by the mistress and buns by Mrs Morice.

1894

12 Jan. School closed this week because of the severity of the weather.

12 Nov. Mr Blackwood, of Willett House, employed four boys for two days 'battue'.

14 Dec. The examination work was well done throughout the week with few exceptions. The infants, too, are mastering their work well. The Revd and Mrs Morice have begun a soup kitchen three days a week for the children attending school.

1895

1 Feb. Weather has been most severe, school closed on Wednesday. Very little work done on Tuesday and Thursday, the cold was so great.

3 May On Thursday the children were given tea by Miss Hawkins, of Whites Farm.

21 June Several of the upper standard absent haymaking.

16 July Many children whortleberry picking this week.

1 August School closed for one month for harvest holiday.

13 Dec. Average attendance 19.6. The embroidery class have worked Christmas cards to take home, each one paying for their own.

24 Dec. Mary Tyzach resigned.

1896

6 Jan. Martha Hannah Gregory re-opened the school.

14 Feb. Punished boy for making marks on the school furniture.

5 March The new Rector, the Revd J.M. Sangar, visited the school.

8 May Martha Gregory resigned.

8 June Alice Wadsworth took charge of the school.

15 June Three girls kept in for careless writing.

29 June Knitting throughout the school unsatisfactory – not one girl capable of knitting a pair of stockings.

30 Oct. Attendance getting very low owing

to so many leaving the parish – only 18 present.

23 Dec. Mrs Sangar and daughters visited and presented the children with books. The mistress gave each child a packet of sweets.

1897

11 Feb. A boy received two strokes with cane for using bad words both in school and outside during the dinner hour. He is a new boy and unruly.

21 June Holiday to celebrate the Diamond Jubilee.

9 July Haymaking in full swing and attendance low because of it.

13 Sept. Two little girls punished for disobedience – one showing a great deal of temper.

1898

3 Jan. School re-opened, only 14 present due to a great deal of sickness in the parish.

31 Jan. The head boy of the school, John Fouracre, withdrawn for work.

10 Feb. Gave several girls a stroke on the hand for calling names after one of their school mates as they left school last night.

21 Feb. Much snow and slippery roads – school closed for two days.

22 April The four Amesburys left this week, reducing the number on the book to 21.

24 June Boy sent into school during dinner for writing rude words on the school porch.

29 June Bible lesson interrupted this morning by inattention and then by the disobedience of B.P., who refused, though told several times, to bring her Bible and sit on the form nearest me. She was given one stroke on her hand and in consequence made a most deafening noise that the lesson had to be stopped. Remained at the end of school to do as she was bid.

29 July Gave results of examinations, giving the kindergarten article to those who have done best in each standard, also to Beatrice Lea for her good sewing.

5 Sept. Commenced school, 20 present. Heat intense, 100 degrees in the sun.

1899

29 May Several away with whooping cough.

7 June Very few children present due to the annual Monksilver Club Walk.

14 July A boy has scarlatina.

22 Sept. Miss Blommart is giving a tea to the children and mothers – school dismissed at 11.30.

15 Dec. Weather rough and wintery. Thursday brought deep snow. Too cold for ordinary lessons – children sat as near the fire as possible with knitting and carol singing, etc.

1900

1 Jan.   School re-commenced, 23 present.

12 Jan.   Children in Standard IV away all week due to influenza.

13–23 Feb. Heavy snow blocking some roads, followed by heavy rain. Illness also greatly affected numbers.

2 March News received of the Relief of Ladysmith – children given a holiday.

17 May   Inspector's report: 'This is an interesting little school. The mistress is an industrious, conscientious teacher and she succeeds in thoroughly securing the attention of her scholars... Grant to be received £53.15s.6d.'

22 May   News of the Relief of Mafeking reached us on Saturday and the children had a day's holiday yesterday (Monday).

28 May   Being a partial eclipse of the sun this afternoon, an object lesson was given upon it, and the children looked at the sun before they went home through smoked glass.

29 May   Being Oak Apple Day, all the children came in wearing oak – improved the occasion by telling them the origin of it.

31 May   News reached the village of the taking of Pretoria. Measles have broken out in the parish.

11 June   Official news of the British flag floating over Pretoria – our day's holiday was premature!

20 July   William Middleton met with an accident in the evening and broke an arm.

5 Sept.   Emma Shepherd, a second class certificated teacher, re-opened school, 12 present.

12 Oct.   Several families left the village, only 23 names on register.

19 Oct.   Several children away this week picking blackberries and potatoes.

3 Dec.   School to be closed for a month due to measles.

1901

20 May   M. Bryant took charge of the school today.

19 July   Several children away whortleberry picking.

11 Sept.   School treat given by Miss Blommart at Willett Farm.

25 Oct.   The children were all present and had their photographs taken.

1902

16 May   Several children away with bad colds, others on account of the Agricultural Show at Wiveliscombe.

24 June   Telegram received at the Rectory stating the Coronation is postponed on account of the King's illness. The feast will take place on Thursday as arranged, but no sports.

24 Dec.   Closed this morning for Christmas holiday. The children were given oranges, sweets and biscuits and those who attended Sunday School each received a book and handkerchief.

1903

1 April   Twenty-two on books, 18 present.

22 June   Only 14 present, several away on account of sheep shearing.

19 Sept.   Several children away on Wednesday on account of Stogumber sports.

1904

15 Feb.   School re-opened after being closed for seven weeks due to scarlatina in the village.

25 April Girl went home during dinner hour because she had been punished in the a.m. for being sulky.

9 Sept.   School closed for Miss Blommart's annual treat.

16 Sept.   Bad attendance all week, several children away on account of weather. Frank Tarr absent all week – rabbiting.

23 Sept.   Drill lessons given this week in accordance with the new syllabus received from County Council.

9 Dec.   Bad colds prevalent throughout the school.

1905

10 Feb.   The results of the quarterly examinations is, on the whole, fairly good. Arithmetic is a little weak, but has improved.

17 Feb.   Girl sent home for having ringworm on her face.

19 May   Half-day holiday on Thursday for the Yeomanry Sports at Crowcombe.

16 June   Report from H.M.I.: 'This little school is being well conducted by Miss Bryant. A globe should be provided.'

23 June   Florence Potter absent owing to a chickenpox outbreak at Vexford.

27 Oct.   Special lesson on Monday for 'Trafalgar Day'.

20 Dec.   School closed for Christmas holidays. Miss Bryant resigned.

1906

8 Jan.   Mary Haddinott took charge.

2 March Florence Potter, a V Standard girl, has left this week to go into service.

4 May   Mary Bartraham attending school at Monksilver – 20 children now on register.

29 June   Spelling continues to be bad in the lower standard. Great attention will have to be given to the subject.

1907

1 March Attendance has been smaller than ever this week. Greta Thorne has crushed her fingers in a mangling machine and is unable to attend school.

31 May   Attendance higher this week than for some time. Teacher thinks that the giving of prizes for regular attendance has led to this improvement.

1908

10 Jan.   Gladys Hoddinott left to attend a secondary school at Taunton.

17 Jan.   Ray Hoddinott has left to attend Williton School – 17 on register.

14 Feb.   Ethel Burnett, aged 12, gave in her name as a candidate for the examination for Labour Certificate.

29 May   Monday being Empire Day, suitable lessons were given and patriotic songs were sung. This morning reference was made to the custom of wearing oak leaves on 29 May.

19 June   Daisy Tarr left school, having reached 14.

25 Sept.   The Milton family are leaving Holcombe Water and are moving to Kings-brompton. Only 13 attending school now.

16 Oct.   The Miltons have gone to Tripp Bottom and Clatworthy will be their nearest school.

1909

22 Jan.   A boy has been absent from school this week and, on questioning his sister as to the cause, was told he had no tidy clothes to wear.

5 March Severe weather with heavy snow on Wednesday has seriously interfered with attendance.

7 May   Gave County Council and other prizes to those children with regular attendance – four children had not missed a single attendance. Ernest Tarr was awarded a prize for good conduct.

3 Sept.   Ethel Burnett left school, having reached 14.

10 Dec.   Exchanged reading books with Monksilver School.

23 Dec.   Tuesday being St Thomas's Day, several children away begging in the village according to a very old custom.

1910

14 Jan.   The Westcombe family have left the village for Stogumber.

28 Jan.   Sent in my resignation today.

11 March An afternoon visit was made by Mr and Mrs Salt, of Hartrow Manor, and their visitors.

18 March A new boy, who has evidently been kept from school a great deal, started today. He is 10, but will have to go into the infant class.

31 March Mary Hoddinott resigned today.

4 April   Winifred Rutt now in charge of school. Admitted Cyril and Leonard Rutt, Herbert and Francis Fouracre and William Stephens.

29 April   William Charles Jones admitted.

3 June   Admitted Elizabeth Joan Mills.

15 July   William Jones has met with an accident and will not be able to come to school for some time.

5 Sept.   School re-commenced. Admitted Maurice A. Hall. Mabel Tarr, being 13 and having good attendance, has left to go to a situation.

1911

19 Jan.   Commenced school. Amelia and George Burnett absent through sickness.

12 June   Admitted Sidney Waterman.

24 Nov.   Only seven children have been present this week, the other 10 are all suffering from whooping cough.

1912

5 Jan.   Closed school at 3.15 pm to allow

children to go to a Christmas treat given by Captain and Mrs Connap at Willett.

18 March School re-opened this morning after being closed for three weeks owing to an outbreak of mumps.

1 April Admitted Louisa Stephens and Edith Mary Stephens.

23 April Admitted Florence Stephens.

13 Sept. Cyril Henly Rutt has left to attend Huish Grammar School. Donald Kerslake has broken his collar bone and is unable to attend school.

7 Oct. Admitted Sydney James, Ella Mary and Ernest Henry Webber.

1913

9 May Attendance poor owing to bad weather.

6 June Admitted Elizabeth Mills.

16 June Admitted Frederick Webber, Arthur Webber and Lillian Prout – 22 on books.

1914

16 Jan. John Tarr, being 15 years of age, left school today.

8 May Edith Stephens is still unfit for school, every other child has been present all week.

25 Sept. Louisa and Florence Stephens are leaving the parish to live at Tolland.

9 Nov. Admitted Albert Stephens and re-admitted Edith Stephens, Elsie Coles and William Coles.

1915

1 April Sidney Waterman has broken his collarbone.

4 June School commenced after the Whitsun holiday. Admitted Maud Webber, Hilda Breed and Herbert Webber.

3 Sept. Leonard Rutt has left to attend Huish Grammar School.

1916

10 Jan. School re-opened after Christmas holiday. Attendance very good at 17 with 18 on the books.

25 Feb. Through the heavy fall of snow only two children arrived at the school. School closed for a week – heavy snow, road from Willett blocked.

22 Sept. Maurice Hall has been granted a fortnight's exemption from school to help on the land.

22 Dec. Only two children came to school on Thursday morning owing to a very heavy snowstorm, so school was closed a day earlier for the Christmas holidays.

1917

2 March Admitted Clifford and Edith Pugsley.

9 March A heavy fall of snow has prevented children reaching school.

25 May Admitted Lucy Webber.

8 June Admitted Albert Thomas Breed.

1918

18 Jan. A heavy fall of snow made the roads impassable and the children could not reach school.

15 April Admitted Frances Waterman.

22 April Admitted Leonard Ware.

19 July William Stephens has been granted permission to leave school to work on the farm.

1919

10 Jan. Sidney Waterman has left to go to work. The Webber family have removed to Williton through the death of their father.

2 May William Stephens returned to school, being recalled from farm work.

4 July Revd J.M. Sangar visited the school.

3 Oct. The afternoon school starts at 1.15 and closes at 3.30 to allow children to reach home before dark.

10 Oct. Revd H. Gardner-McTaggart visited the school.

1920

29 March Ronald Gooding has been away all week with croup.

16 April Admitted Olive May and Florence Horsey.

7 May George Ware and the Stephens family have been away all week through sickness.

1921

8 April Admitted Doris Horsey.

6 May Ronald Gooding has left school this afternoon; he starts on Monday at the Modern School at Minehead.

22 Aug. School re-opened after the summer holidays. Admitted Wilbert Parsons; 25 on books. Dorothy and Albert Rexworthy are away through illness.

2 Sept. Admitted Gordon Edwin Hayes.

26 Sept. Admitted Gerald Thomas Webber.

1922

10 Feb. Examined registers, found same correct – H. Gardner-McTaggart.

2 June Admitted Albert Ralph Curtis.

8 Sept. School re-opened after summer holidays. Admitted Rex Webber.

17 Nov. The children were given a holiday on Friday on account of the Parish Festival.

1923

9 Feb. Admitted Phyllis Irene Burston.

16 Feb. Dennis Fox has been absent all week with toothache.

13 April Admitted John Stephens and Grace Horsey.

27 July The children had their annual outing to Minehead.

3 Aug. Rex Webber is now 14 and leaves today to commence work.

10 Nov. William Coles, who was 14 in August, has left school this week to commence work on a farm.

1924

7 Jan. School re-opened after Christmas holidays. Miss Walland commenced duty as a monitress; 25 on books.

11 April Report from the Diocesan Inspector: 'This little school, containing children of all ages, is very cleverly instructed by

the head teacher, and she manages to secure the interest of all... A very happy and well-disciplined school. The school is classed as excellent.'

23 May A boy is being treated by Dr Webb for ringworm on the body and cannot attend school.

4 June Examined registers and found same correct – H. Gardner-McTaggart.

31 Oct. Albert Stephens and Clarice Fox, having reached 14 years, left last night.

1925

9 Jan. Admitted Stanley James Carter.

20 June Beatrice Breed was appointed monitress by the managers.

25 April Admitted Frank Chapman. Gerald Webber is leaving to attend Brompton School owing to the distance.

8 June Admitted Margaret Cridland.

26 June Stanley Carter was absent on Friday carrying hay.

1926

26 March Robert Stephens has developed mumps.

14 May Frank Chapman is home with mumps.

2 July Annual outing to Minehead.

1 Oct. D.F. was sent home at 1.30, being wet through. In playing leap-frog in the meadow he accidentally fell into the water.

3 Dec. Miss Beatrice Breed has today resigned her appointment as monitress.

17 Dec. Miss Phyllis Davis was appointed monitress.

1927

28 Jan. The Revd H. Gardner-McTaggart and his two sons came to say goodbye to the children. They presented each child with a box of chocolates.

17 June Admitted Hilda Thore Marshall.

29 July The Revd Oswald de Bloque visited the school.

16 Dec. Only eight children are able to attend school owing to chickenpox.

1928

8 June Admitted Elsie Kent.

1 Aug. Annual outing to Weston-super-Mare.

8 Sept. Admitted Edmund Welsh and Frederick Keates.

1929

27 May Olive Mabel Davis commenced work this morning in place of her sister, who resigned to take up nursing.

23 Sept. Admitted George, Mary and Dorothy Poole.

30 Sept. Admitted Peter Rutt.

25 Oct. Robert Stephens left today to commence work, being 14 years.

1930

6 Jan. Florence Horsey has left and taken a situation at Stogumber.

21 Feb. George Poole has broken a leg and will be absent for some time.

18 July Grace Horsey has been successful

Elworthy School, 1928.

in Part II of the 'free place' examination and will begin her secondary education at Bishop Fox's School in September.

1931

19 June   Benjamin Keates is in Minehead Hospital with a fractured leg.

31 July   Doris Horsey finishes... and Margaret Cridland commences at Bishop Fox's School in September, having gained a 'free place' scholarship.

1 Sept.   Admitted Jean Rexworthy.

29 Oct.   Winifred Rutt resigned charge of Elworthy School today.

3 Nov.   School re-opened after half-term holiday with 13 on the register and all present. I took charge of this school in place of Mrs Rutt, who has retired after 21 years in this school – May Gertrude White.

2 Dec.   At recess time, with the permission of the managers, I took the children up to Elworthy Cross to a meet of the foxhounds.

1932

22 Jan.   John Stephens has been absent all week, both of his parents and brothers are ill with influenza.

5 Feb.   Only five present today.

13 April   Admitted Vera Hooper, an infant, who has attended Brompton Ralph Council School.

5 May   Report from Diocesan Inspector re religious instruction: 'The children have been excellently taught and it was a pleasure to find the Old and New Testaments and Catechism so carefully linked together. The singing has much improved... and the school in regard to religious knowledge as a whole is very good.' – Phoebe M. Rees.

29 July   I resign my charge of this school today – May G. White.

12 Sept.   There are no chairs in the school for the use of the staff. Chairs were borrowed from one of the farms for medical inspection by Dr Parke.

1 Nov.   I took charge of this school today – Edith Badman.

28 Nov.   John Stephens absent with toothache.

1933

19 Jan.   Received half a ton of coal today.

26 Jan.   School closed until 6 February, six children absent with influenza.

6 Feb.   School re-opened – Frederick Keates, Bertie Keates and Vera Hooper absent with influenza.

24 Feb.   School closed – bad weather, snow very deep.

25 April   School re-opened this morning with 16 children present. Admitted Doreen, Beatrice and Dennis Bawden and Douglas Keates.

26 April   B.B. and J.R. absent this morning – too tired to attend after a late night!

28 April   Miss Davis left the school today to take up nursing.

1 May   Admitted Cecil Bawden this morning.

5 May   A girl absent this morning – had to look after the younger children at home while her mother went to buy boots for the school-children.

9 May   Health visitor called and inspected the children's heads – all found clean.

21 July   School outing to Burnham-on-Sea.

21 Sept.   Admitted Margaret Baker.

2 Oct.   Admitted Molly and Edward Phillips.

9 Oct.   Admitted Gilbert and Raymond Chaplin.

1934

16 Jan.   Miss Mary Hutchings commenced duties as monitress.

2 Feb.   Captain Fitzgerald, physical training organiser, called this morning.

29 Nov.   The school is closed today for the Royal Wedding.

21 Dec.   The school closed at 12 noon today

to enable the children to go to Taunton for their Christmas treat.

1935

11 March Only two children present owing to heavy snow.

6 May   School closed for the Jubilee celebrations.

31 May   Miss Hutchings left the school...

1 July   Leonard Stephens was enrolled this morning.

4 Nov.   Hilda Rexworthy was enrolled this morning.

6 Nov.   The school closed today for the Royal Wedding.

1936

10 Jan.   Revd F.S. Stothers, Rector of Monksilver and Elworthy, called today.

28 Jan.   School was closed all day for the funeral of His Majesty King George V. Children listened to the service broadcast from Windsor Chapel at the school house.

28 Feb.   I resigned my charge of this school today – Edith A. Badman.

9 March I, Emmeline Crump, take charge of this school today. Twenty-seven children present.

6 July   Owing to very wet weather, only 13 children present.

1 Sept.   Miss Horsey commenced duties here as monitress.

30 Nov.   I resign my charge of this school today – Emmeline Crump.

1 Dec.   I, N. Bacon, take charge, temporarily, of this school today.

1937

11 Jan.   School re-opened – number on books 19.

29 Jan.   School closed today owing to heavy snow.

14 June   Mrs Bacon, having broken down in health, failed to arrive for duty. I, Edith N. Long, commenced this morning temporary teaching service at this school.

Subscribers

Ronald Conibeer Adams, Williton, Somerset
Heather Venn Van Almelo, Cape Town,
    South Africa
Margaret Armstrong, Chelmsford, Essex
Peter and Betty Armstrong, Trull, Taunton
Mr Darby Ash, Stogumber, Somerset
Mrs B.A. Atkins, Tolland, Somerset
Tim Auton, Bishops Lydeard (eldest son of
    Anne Auton née Notley)
Robert and Angela Bendall, Huish Moor,
    Somerset
Robin Bex, Portishead, North Somerset
Ann and Keith Bishop, Williton, Somerset
Harold Braben, Monksilver 1940–47
Michael Brandon, Denchworth, Oxon
Judy Elisabeth Brewer, Yarde, Somerset
David Bryant, Vellow, Stogumber,
    Somerset
Gerald Bull, Bishops Lydeard
Linda and David Butcher, Stogumber,
    Somerset
K.J. Calloway, Taunton, Somerset
Sharon Campbell, Stogumber, Somerset
David A. Cavell, Cardiff, Wales
Mike and Wendy Chapman, Yeovil,
    Somerset
Roy and Helen Chave, Watchet, Somerset
Benjamin P. Cheek, Nettlecombe, Somerset
Lance P. Cheek, Nettlecombe, Somerset
James Chidgey, Banstead, Surrey
Maurice and Joyce Chidgey, Watchet,
    Somerset
Vera Chidgey (née Hooper),
    Williton/formerly Monksilver
Lisa Chidgey and Steve and Ethan Plenty,
    Alcombe, Somerset
Maureen M. Clarke, Torre, Somerset
Sheila C. Clavey (née Calloway), Watchet
Nicholas and Dawn Marie Coltman,
    Monksilver

Michael and Kathleen Cooke,
    Beggearnhuish, Somerset
Mr R.A. and Mrs V.H. Cosens, Stogumber,
    Somerset
Rosemary Cox M.B.E., Willett House
Susan A. Crane (née Symes), Ickenham,
    Middlesex
Gavin Criddle, Altona, Victoria, Australia
Jeremy M. Danson, Stogumber, Somerset
Lewis Jack Davey
Raymond Davis, Colchester, Essex
Denis Davis, Minehead, Somerset
Paul Davis, Bristol
Mr Roy Dennett, London SW4
Annette and Samuel Dickinson and Lee
    Graham, Exeter, Devon
Margaret Dring, Stogumber, Somerset
Audrey and David Emery, Northam Mill,
    Stogumber
Graham Evans, Carlton, Victoria, Australia
Anne Evans (née Criddle), Carlton, Victoria,
    Australia
Mr Paul Eveleigh, Chalford, Stroud
Keith and Molly Farmer, Bicknoller,
    Somerset
Philip and Sheila Gibbs, Wick House,
    Stogumber
Simon Gillett, Tarr
Mr and Mrs J. Gostling
Mrs Flossie Hall (née Moore),
    Monksilver/Williton, Somerset
Mrs M.F. Hann
Joan and George Hardie, Bishops Lydeard
Bruce, Helen and Julian Harding,
    Stogumber, Somerset
Patricia A. Hardwick, Stogumber, Somerset
R.J.N. Hayes, Stogumber, Somerset
Geoff and Chris Hayes
Ron and Honor Hayes, Stogumber,
    Somerset

Robert J.N. Hayes, Taranaki, Stogumber

Michael J. Hayes, Stogumber, Somerset

Dale A. Headington, Sarnau, Powys

Arthur and Beryl Headington (née Hayes), Sarnau, Powys

Kathleen V. Heath, Old School House, Elworthy

Barry and Jenny Hibbert

Brian Hicks, Cookham, Berkshire

Carole C. Hill, Williton, Somerset

Gordon R. Hobbs, Keynsham, Bristol

Audrey Holcombe (née Pearce)

Mr and Mrs S.G. Hopwood, Thatched Cottage, Yarde, Somerset

Vivian Horn, Stogumber 1948–64

Sheila D. Hubbard, formerly of Stogumber

June and Roger Hutchings, Dene View, Stogumber

B. Jewell

Colin Jones, formerly of Stogumber

Paul Jones, formerly of Stogumber

Rodney Gerald Jones, Taunton, Somerset

Joan G. Jones, Watchet, Somerset

J. Rachel Kelly, Capton, Somerset

Winifred Kingsbury, Weacombe, Somerset

The Revd Brian W. Kirk, Stogumber, Somerset

Stella Knifton, Bexhill-on-Sea, East Sussex

Sharon Koppa (née Jones), Holford, Somerset

Michael C. Langdon, Clayhidon, Devon

Roy Lawrence, Stogumber, Somerset

Michael Leat, Bristol

Rosemary M. Lewis, Bristol

Robert and Mary Lintott, Nettlecombe, Somerset

Mrs Doris Lock, Williton/formerly Stogumber

Percy E. and Stella G. Long, Williton, Somerset

Laura Longworth, Monksilver, Somerset

Frances Longworth, Monksilver, Somerset

Robina Longworth, Monksilver, Somerset

Revd Ian and Monica Mallard, Watchet, Somerset

Phyllis Marley, Bampton, Devon

Cherry Mawer (née corfield), Nettlecombe Rectory 1939–1950

Gerald May, Lydenburg, South Africa

Edwin May, Williton, Somerset

Ian McCann, Old Cleeve, Somerset

Isabel Molland, Colehill, Dorset

John and Joyce Montagnon, Monksilver

Philip Barry Moore, Monksilver, Somerset

Sandra J. Moore, Watchet (Willett), Somerset

Rachel J. Moores, Bristol

Lesley Morgan, Little Orchard, Stogumber

Gloria Nash, Higher Vellow, Stogumber

Steve and Jan Nash, Monksilver, Somerset

Nick and Jackie Nation, Lydeard St Lawrence, Somerset

P. Nicholson, Lydeard St Lawrence, Somerset

Mr and Mrs P.M. Notley, Monksilver

Mervyn and Angela Orchard-Lisle, Monksilver

Lucy Parrott, daughter of Ronald Hosegood, Washford

The Parsons Family, Monksilver

Mr R.W. Penny, Stogumber

Camilla Perry (née Moore), Triscombe, Somerset

Nigel and Sue Pike, Bilbrook, Somerset

Hector Potter, Belle Vue, St Audries

David and Lynda Powell, Cardiff

Anne Preston-Littlewood, Monksilver, Somerset

Michael G. Ray, Cambridge

Heather Rich, Bridgwater, Somerset

Geoff Rowbotham, Monksilver (Wartime evacuee)

Ann Sanders, (Bex) Corfe, Somerset

Jim Sansom, Escott, Stogumber, Somerset

Jean Scott, Lydeard St Lawrence, Somerset

Audrey Scrace (née Jones), Williton, Somerset

Dr and Mrs Jonathan Secker-Walker, Stogumber

Sellick Family, Escott Farm, Stogumber

Kathy and Mike Shadrack, Chingford, London

Sylvia M. Sharp (née Calloway), Minehead

C.P. Sharp OBE, Maulden, Bedfordshire

Shirley J. Shorney, Wellington, Somerset

Beryl A. Simms, Stogumber, Somerset

B. and J. Skudder, Doniford

Sorel Small (née Corfield), Nettlecombe

Michael W. Somerfield, Williton, Somerset

Rod and Christine Somerfield, Watchet, Somerset

Adrian Somerfield, Wiveliscombe, Somerset

Joanne Somerfield, Earsham, Bungay, Suffolk

Brian Somerfield, Willett and Higher Vexford

Iain Somerfield-Wade, Garnant, Amanford, Carmarthenshire

Myfanwy V. Squires (Langdon), Pontyclun

Mr Ken Stephens, Williton, Somerset

Francis Stevens, Watchet

Mr Brian G. Stevens, East Quantoxhead/formerly Monksilver

Mr Frank Stevens, Founder of The Esplanade Club, Watchet, circa 1976

Valerie M. Stevens, Williton/formerly Monksilver

Shirley Ann Sully, Williton, Somerset

Mrs Audrey Takel, Fairfield, Willow Grove, Washford, Somerset

Peter Talbot, "Sunnydene" Hill Street, Stogumber, Taunton

Ms Ruth Sara Tayles, Woodford Cottage, Woodford, Somerset, from 1995

John H. Thompson, Stogumber, Somerset

Keith and Joy Towells, Watchet, Somerset

George Tuckfield, Maidenhead, Berkshire

Barbara Vearncombe (née Somerfield), Lydeard St Lawrence

F. Ruth Wallace, Stogumber, Somerset

John F.W. Walling, Newton Abbot, Devon

Hilary and Phil Watts, 'Meadowsweet', Monksilver

Michael and Enyde Webb, Escott, Somerset

Stephen Webb, Shirley and Lewis Roland

Janice K.N. Weetch, Pound Orchard, Crowcombe

A.G. West, Stogumber

Jim and Jean White, Capton, Somerset

Peter M. White, formerly of Williton, Somerset

Robin J. Wichard, Yarde, Somerset

Janet and John Wilkinson, Sutton Coldfield

Joan Williams, Bishops Lydeard, Taunton, Somerset

Peter and Anne Williamson,

Rosa M. Willis, Wellington, Somerset

John Wilson, Monksilver, Somerset

Heather and Mark Wilson, Crowcombe, Somerset

Dr and Mrs David Yates, Higher Vexford

Bruce and Jill Young, Stogumber

Community Histories

❦

The Book of Addiscombe • Canning & Clyde Road Residents Association & Friends
The Book of Addiscombe, Vol. II • Canning & Clyde Road Residents Association & Friends
The Book of Axminster with Kilmington • Les Berry
and Gerald Gosling
The Book of Bampton • Caroline Seward
The Book of Barnstaple • Avril Stone
The Book of Barnstaple, Vol. II • Avril Stone
The Book of The Bedwyns • The Bedwyn History Society
The Book of Bickington • Stuart Hands
Blandford Forum: A Millennium Portrait • Blandford Town Council
The Book of Bramford • Bramford Local History Group
The Book of Breage & Germoe • Stephen Polglase
The Book of Bridestowe • R. Cann
The Book of Bridport • Rodney Legg
The Book of Brixham • Frank Pearce
The Book of Buckfastleigh • Sandra Coleman
The Book of Buckland Monachorum & Yelverton • Hemery
The Book of Carharrack • Carharrack Old Cornwall Society
The Book of Carshalton • Stella Wilks and Gordon Rookledge
The Parish Book of Cerne Abbas • Vale and Vale
The Book of Chagford • Ian Rice
The Book of Chapel-en-le-Frith • Mike Smith
*The Book of Chittlehamholt with
Warkleigh & Satterleigh* • Richard Lethbridge
The Book of Chittlehampton • Various
The Book of Colney Heath • Bryan Lilley
The Book of Constantine • Moore and Trethowan
The Book of Cornwood & Lutton • Compiled by the People of the Parish
The Book of Creech St Michael • June Small
The Book of Cullompton • Compiled by the People of the Parish
The Book of Dawlish • Frank Pearce
*The Book of Dulverton, Brushford,
Bury & Exebridge* • Dulverton & District Civic Society
The Book of Dunster • Hilary Binding
The Book of Edale • Gordon Miller
The Ellacombe Book • Sydney R. Langmead
The Book of Exmouth • W.H. Pascoe
The Book of Grampound with Creed • Bane and Oliver
The Book of Hayling Island & Langstone • Rogers
The Book of Helston • Jenkin with Carter
The Book of Hemyock • Clist and Dracott
The Book of Herne Hill • Patricia Jenkyns
The Book of Hethersett • Hethersett Society Research Group
The Book of High Bickington • Avril Stone
The Book of Ilsington • Dick Wills
The Book of Kingskerswell • Carsewella Local History Group
The Book of Lamerton • Ann Cole & Friends
Lanner, A Cornish Mining Parish • Sharron
Schwartz and Roger Parker
The Book of Leigh & Bransford • Malcolm Scott
The Book of Litcham with Lexham & Mileham • Litcham Historical & Amenity Society
The Book of Loddiswell • Reg and Betty Sampson
The New Book of Lostwithiel • Barbara Fraser
The Book of Lulworth • Rodney Legg
The Book of Lustleigh • Joe Crowdy
The Book of Lyme Regis • Rodney Legg
The Book of Manaton • Compiled by the People of the Parish
The Book of Markyate • Markyate Local History Society
The Book of Mawnan • Mawnan Local History Group
The Book of Meavy • Pauline Hemery
The Book of Minehead with Alcombe • Binding and Stevens

For details of any of the above titles or if you are
interested in writing your own history, please contact: Commissioning Editor Community Histories, Halsgrove House,
Lower Moor Way, Tiverton Business Park, Tiverton, Devon EX16 6SS, England; tel: 01884 259636;
email: katyc@halsgrove.com